The Runaway Climbers
Part 1
How The 2008 K2 Disaster Unfolded

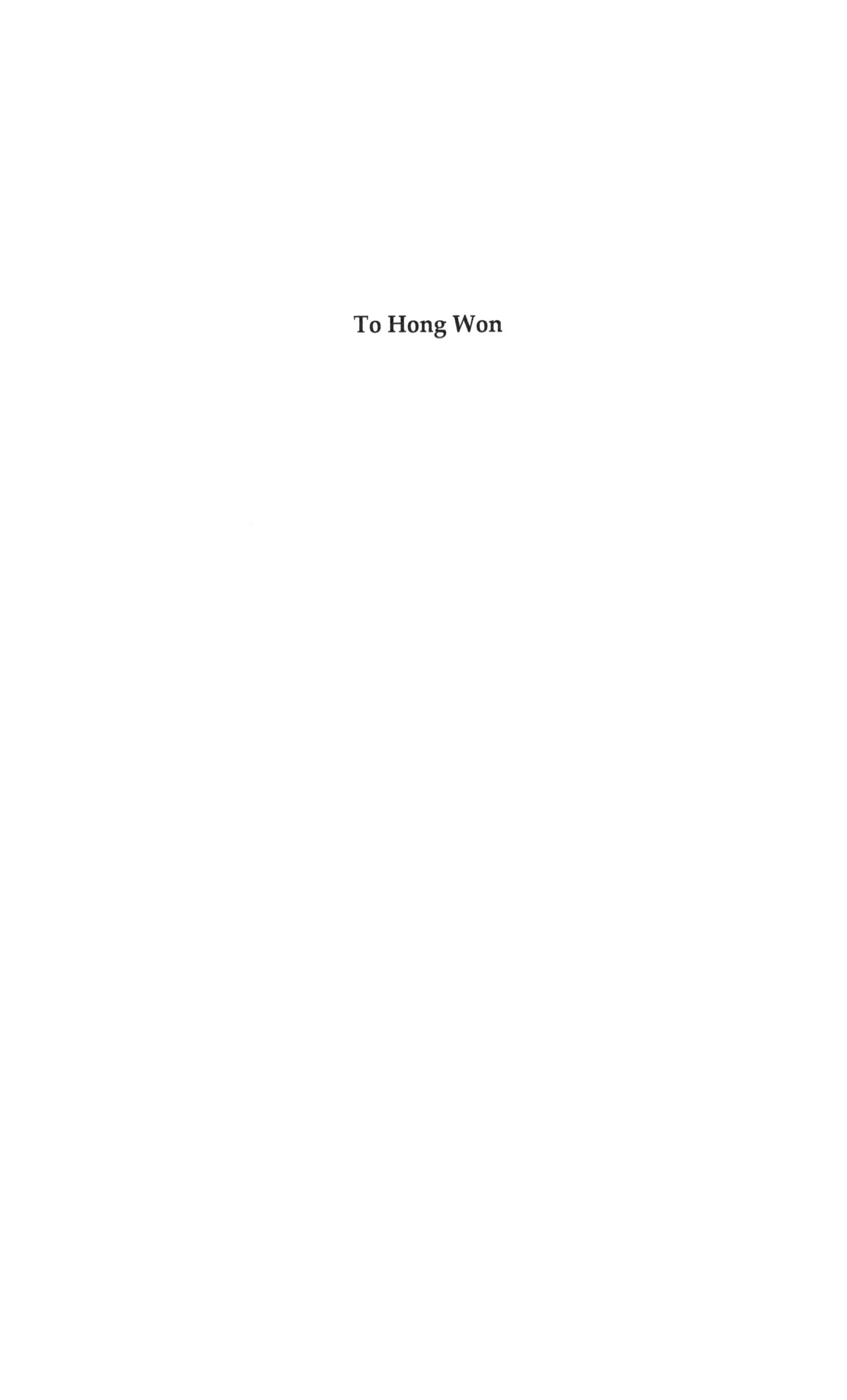
To Hong Won

One

It was June 7, 2008. Four Dutch climbers Wilco, Cas, Roeland and Jelle[1] climbed to Camp 1 again and pitched their tents. They then started to climb toward Camp 2 to install the remaining rope.

The route between Camp 1 and Camp 2 was different from the route taken from Base Camp to Camp 1[2]. They had reached the edge of a high, straight rock tower so they needed to look up for choices and decide whether to directly climb the precipice or journey around the entire tower.

They could have climbed upward. But this choice would expose them to the risk of an avalanche. Going around required the use of more ropes to secure the horizontal section. But, going around looked the better option. They took it.

The 250m sections[3] were places where a high climbing technique was needed. Below their feet was a dazzling 1000m vertical drop.

They passed the traverse section and climbed toward the gully, scrambling up its right side. Layers of snow covered the slope and made it hard to grip with the crampon. It would have been easier when the snow first fell but now the ice had hardened like rock, the slope was slippery and dangerous. New layers of powdered snow covered it.

June 8 B-team members Gerard, Pemba, Mark and Court climbed to Camp 1[4] and dumped their gear there. On the way down to K2 Base Camp (K2BC), a big avalanche began above them. Court disappeared in the snow cloud. When it cleared, his teammates saw him reappear. They sighed with relief after this overwhelming experience.

---

[1] http://vimeo.com/1418206

[2] www.youtube.com/watch?v=z2kKHglj3UA

[3] www.youtube.com/watch?v=0UlAG2ini2o&list=UU7DHYV7rArzfZh U4rK_Nsow

[4] www.youtube.com/watch?v=Dnhcf_kz7WU

The next day, they changed the team's role. At 5am, B-team members started to climb again toward Camp 1, ferrying ropes, tents and the other gear. Gerard and Pemba arrived at Camp 1 first, where they improved the 100m route toward Camp 2. Mark and Court arrived exhausted. The lack of oxygen at that altitude had already threatened the climbers' mental health. This was another of the mountain's harsh realities.

While the B-team members were descending back to K2 Base Camp for food and water, the A-team members arrived at Camp 1, intending to spend the night there to acclimatize.

That night, the Dutch soccer team was playing against Italy. It was the first match for the teams in the European Soccer Championships. An interesting game for the Dutch members![5]

June 9 Since the weather had turned ugly, everyone got to climb down to K2BC. Being stuck in K2 Base Camp was boring. To boost the team's morale they played board games and read books, which were excellent ways of keeping up their spirits.

The team kept the blog. Teammates would take it in turns to post on a daily basis. The blog was a way of keeping climbers connected to their families and friends in the outside world.

The last time they climbed, Mark was lucky to be alive.

"A rock had fallen at break-neck speed!"

Rock fall was one of the dangers in K2 climbing. It was a sensitive issue for climbers.

Wilco van Rooijen was 42 years old, and the team leader had already challenged K2 twice without reaching summit—in 1995 and 2006. K2 had been a lifelong obsession and his crowning goal. During the 1995 K2 Expedition, he was hit by a rock and evacuated by chopper. One of his current team members, 37-year-old Gerard McDonnell was also hit on the head by a rock during his challenge of Broad Peak in 2006. A chopper also evacuated him.

Given Mark's experience, the team analyzed that traversing while someone was above and heading toward Camp 2 posed a risk.[6] They decided to adjust their plan.

K2 is a great and high mountain[7] located on the border of Pakistan and China. At 8611m, K2 is the second highest in the world after

---

[5] http://wwww.summitpost.org/the-norit-s/565473/c-565466

[6] https://www.flickr.com/photos/25037111@N07/2563704637/

Everest (8848m). However, K2 was technically difficult and the hardest prize to earn among the Himalayan Mountains.

Norit International Expedition was the first team to arrive at K2 in the 2008 season. On May 29 this dream team consisting of eight members nested into their resting place at K2 Base Camp.[8] At 5000m, this place was safe from avalanches. Since then, the team had been undertaking step-by-step acclimatization and route works on the Cesen (or S.S.E Spur) route (*see* p. 118).

June 11 The French TGW K2 Expedition arrived at K2BC. This trio comprised Yannick, Patrick, and Christian. Some of Norit's team members visited the French team for a chat.

"Welcome to K2, mates!"

They heard the French were going to challenge the West Face of K2 in alpine style. A bold plan! So their climb would be long and painful.

Still, a number of climbers were on their way in K2BC. Some had just arrived at Islamabad or Skardu while other streams of porters, trekkers and climbers were already marching towards K2. While heading to Concordia, they would hear a famous rumor that Bin Laden was hiding on the mountain.

Strong winds were forecast, and would blow from Sunday. So Norit team leader Wilco was in a hurry to carry out his new plan. But no one foresaw a problem with this plan.

June 12 Wilco and Team-1 members arrived at Camp 2 at 6200m.[9] Jelle arrived an hour later looking exhausted. He described his climb:

> "With the huge load (gas, hooks, 50m climbing rope, snow stakes, sleeping bag) on my back I was having difficulty with breathing. Every 5 to 10 steps I had to stop to get some air in my lungs."

Camp 2 site was such a small place it only permitted them to set up two tents.[10] While they were waiting for Mark and Roeland, they shoveled

---

[7] http://en.wikipedia.org/wiki/K2

[8] www.youtube.com/watch?v=Ef8wUwERTwI&list=UU7DHYV7rArzfZh U4rK_Nsow&index=6

[9] www.youtube.com/watch?v=7ZYTzWiA-hw

[10] www.youtube.com/watch?v=I95OK3zGK50

to make the platform and secured the tents.[11] After two hours of this, they prepared soup and tea.

For Roeland and Jelle, it was the first night. They were going to sleep at an altitude of 6000m. Mark had continuing stomach problems, possibly caused by the altitude. He couldn't digest food and would often vomit during the night.

Norit team had another base camp at Netherland, called Netherland Base Camp (NLBC). The base camp manager of NLBC was Maarten van Eck, who was a webmaster. He had been busy supporting the K2 climbers weekly by recapping what had happened in K2BC and planning for the new move. He would play an important role in the 2008 K2 season.

Maarten searched an Internet site to verify the time difference. Between K2BC and NLBC it was four hours—for instance, if it was 1500 hr in Amsterdam it would be 1900 hr at K2.

---

[11] http://vimeo.com/1418255

Two

June 14 Team-1 members set out to climb as high as they could. They hoped to reach the Shoulder so they could take on the next stage, which was the summit push.

"Oh no, the rope's run out!"

There was no more rope to secure the last section. Rope shortage was a problem they had not foreseen and it was an embarrassing moment for the Norit team.

It meant not only that they couldn't make the attack but also they couldn't set up any other tactics. A way of solving the problem was to secure rope from somewhere.

As soon as they got to K2 Base Camp, they contacted their travel agency to ask for help. The agency decided the Skardu support team would deliver 600m of extra rope by porter. But how long would the rope take to arrive to K2 Base Camp from Skardu?

June 15 Around 3pm, a large expedition arrived at K2BC. It was the Korean K2 Expedition. They started to set up their tents at 4900m, a few yards away from Norit.[12]

Meanwhile, Gerard of the Norit team had kept up his soul-searching on the rope problem.

'How could this rope shortage occur?'[13]

Wilco had also brainstormed the matter. And he posted an idea on the team's blog.

---

[12] https://www.flickr.com/photos/25037111@N07/2607536328/in/photostream/

[13] http://www.humanedgetech.com/expedition/mcdonnell/index.php?dispid=11&view=0

"In fact it is the lack of other expeditions that's causing the rope problem. Normally expeditions share ropes and are appointing who is responsible for certain sections on the mountain."

It was strange, blaming their rope problem on the lack of other expeditions. It was too early for other climbers, to address the problem in that way. Wilco finally saw a solution and decided to use the Korean team. Maarten[14] also described what happened:

"Wilco arranged a meeting today with the Korean Expedition leader. The S.S.E route and the Abruzzi route join high on the mountain. Wilco will ask the Koreans to use some of their ropes to fix that part of the combined route."

However, Wilco was unlucky. It was difficult for him to get his point across to the newly arrived climbers because the Korean team leader, Kim Jae-Su, and another rising star Ms Go Mi-Young had not yet arrived. They were the main decision-makers of the Korean team. The current team, called the "advance team", could not make decisions without their say-so.

While another Kim (Seong-Sang, 48), who had kept a low profile, had been leading the advance team up to K2 Base Camp, forty-five year-old Hwang Dong-Jin would lead the climb. Hwang was a good 8000m climber and one of the more well-known of the Himalayan climbing community. In the team were two more senior members and five junior members. The seniors were ex-lawyer Lee Won-Seup and female climber Song Ki-Hwa. The juniors were Shon Byung-Woo, Kim Hyo-Gyeong, Park Kyeong-Hyo, Lee Seung-Rok and Kim Tae-Gyu.

June 16 It was raining at K2BC. The Norit team explained the scientific and graphic aspects of their weather forecasting in their blog.[15] They also introduced their team's meteorologist Abbas. He had advanced computer equipment, which could analyze the K2 weather.[16] This was a secret weapon to show off the team's strength.

---

[14] https://www.flickr.com/photos/25037111@N07/2720128425/

[15] https://www.flickr.com/photos/25037111@N07/2719706414/in/photostream/

[16] https://www.flickr.com/photos/25037111@N07/2718658169/in/photostream/

June 17

"We can provide some ropes!"

The Norit team received two further responses about the rope problem. One came from an Italian team and another from an American team. They were responding to Norit's blog. Norit members rejoiced and replied, "United ropes of the World!"

However, when would it arrive at K2 Base Camp?

Three

June 18 Other climbers, Hugues and Nick, arrived to K2 Base Camp. They were a part of an international assembly of climbers. It became a French-led international team. Sixty-one-year-old Hugues from the French team was the nominal leader. His twenty-three year-old American member Nick Rice would be the youngest climber in the 2008 K2 season.

After setting up their tents at 5000m, they went down to greet the Norit camp, which had not yet decided on the route they would take.

At 3pm, the members of the Serbian K2 Vojvodina Expedition also arrived at K2BC. They decided to set up their base camp at 5150m, which was only a few meters higher than the Norit team. With their tents pitched and their national flag in the ground, they held a brief arrival ceremony. Their travel agency presented a goat to the team.

The Serbian team consisted of five Serb members, three Pakistani high altitude porters (Haps) and two kitchen staff.[17] The names of the Serb members were Iso Planic, Predrag Zagorac, Dren Mandic, Milivoj Erdeljan and their team leader Miodrag Jovovic, who had not yet arrived at K2BC.

The Serbian team chose the Abruzzi route, the same route taken by the Koreans. It was the variation spur of the Abruzzi route, also known as the South East Spur (*see* p. 118). This was the normal route to K2, first taken by an Italian team to lead them to the top of K2 in 1954.

The route was technically demanding and dangerous. First, the infamous risk in this route was rock fall. The route has also been called Rock Spur. Second, the hardest part on this route is the Black Pyramid section because it consisted of many exposed rocks and ice.

The Serbian team's climbing schedule was similar to the Korean's. They preferred to set up high camps before July 13, and then attempt the first summit push on around July 18 when the full moon was expected.

---

[17] www.youtube.com/watch?v=YfSX9NTJpSQ&list=UU2WKgh_p268Mg
61-7fIaa7A&index=16

They had no time to lose. However, the snowy weather[18][19] hampered most of the climbers, forcing them to stay at K2BC. [20] Neighboring mountains K2 and the Broad Peak were covered in thick mist.

Despite of the weather, the Korean team set up the Advance Base Camp (ABC) at 5300m. It was located over the Abruzzi Close, reached after passing the left side of the icefall section in the Godwin-Austen glacier. They stocked up on supplies at ABC. Step-by-step, they would ferry the food and other gear to the upper camps.

June 21 The sun came out. K2 revealed itself in all of its beauty. It boosted climbers' morale.

For the Serbian team, it was the first climbing day. They were going to climb up to the ABC. On the way up, they saw the human remains of climbers who had died during the K2 climb years earlier. When they got to the ABC, Korean team members welcomed them and suggested that they could share their team's tents.

It was an easy warm-up for them. So Predja posted the day's climbing on their blog:

> "And then—surprise! Our carriers suggested that we start with rope fixing to C1 immediately because weather is good and clear. We filled good on 5.300m and accepted. Way to C1 goes aboard one big snowy mountainside and it is fresh streak of one avalanche. It was all the snow from days before today and it is comparatively safely for climbing. In the beginning scarp is 30°. Afterwards scarp is bigger and bigger . . . 45° . . . 50° . . . 55° . . . Easier part we passed together. On 5.600m it was the end of ropes. Rest of ropes we will install some other day."

The team also uploaded their climb on YouTube.[21] On the same day, Korean team leader Kim Jae-Su, aged forty-eight, and the woman star

---

[18] www.youtube.com/watch?v=_mNFxZKkLJ8&index=15&list =UU2WKgh_p268Mg61-7fIaa7A

[19] www.youtube.com/watch?v=4_zCo0t4Dcc&index=13&list=UU2WKgh_ p268Mg61-7fIaa7A

[20] www.youtube.com/watch?v=7jj0uIJdwHw&list=UU2WKgh_ p268Mg61-7fIaa7A&index=14

[21] www.youtube.com/watch?v=jfk0BAhD8No&index=11&list=UU2WKgh _p268Mg61-7fIaa7A

climber Go Mi-Young, aged forty-one, flew in with their Sherpa team and landed at Karakorum. They then arrived at the K2 Base Camp.

The Korean teams assembled into the 2008 Flying Jump Korea K2 Expedition. With seventeen members, it was the largest team in K2BC.

June 22 In the morning, there was a loud groaning sound. It was Imran Ahmed, a Pakistani liaison officer for the French International Expedition. He had been suffering altitude sickness from day one in K2 Base Camp, which eventually developed into lung edema (water in his lung).

The Serbian team helped him with medicine. Qudrat and Karim from the Hugues' Haps and the other Haps from the Serbian team helped the mission to evacuate him to the military base at Concordia,[22] where several glacial streams converge. It was an unusual mission and a kindness from the Serbian team.

On the same day, Kim had visited the Serbian team for a chat, and he suggested to the team that they unite to install fixed ropes so they could climb and summit together

The Serbs were glad about this suggestion and the team posted it on their blog without proper understanding of Kim's name and position:

> "We are satisfied that Mr. Kim Ye So (president of Korean climbing federation) said that we can install fix-ropes and climbing and summit together. We have good experience with Koreans (summit G1 & G2 last years) and it is good combination for us."

---

[22] http://www.nickrice.us/index_files/k2dispatch24.htm

Four

Kim had a grand agenda. It was the women's fourteen 8000er race. He had typically hurried the team's climbing progress on the Himalaya's big mountains, and now he wanted to bag K2 by making the summit push on July 18.

To do this, he first wanted the ropes fixed on the route as soon as possible in a team effort. And second, he wanted help from the Haps to navigate, especially on the route of the summit pyramid section.

Then, what was the women's fourteen 8000er race? As we know, there are fourteen peaks over 8000m in the world. All these peaks are in the Himalayas.[23]

1.	Everest	8848m	Nepal/China (Tibet)
2.	K2	8611	Pakistan/China
3.	Kangchenjunga	8586	Nepal/India
4.	Lhotse	8516	Nepal/China (Tibet)
5.	Makalu	8463	Nepal/China (Tibet)
6.	Cho Oyu	8201	Nepal/China (Tibet)
7.	Dhaulagiri	8167	Nepal
8.	Manaslu	8163	Nepal
9.	Nanga Parbat	8126	Pakistan
10.	Annapurna	8091	Nepal
11.	Gasherbrum I	8068	Pakistan/China
12.	Broad Peak	8047	Pakistan/China
13.	Gasherbrum II	8035	Pakistan/China
14.	Shishapangma	8027	China (Tibet)

The Italian climber Reinhold Messner (born 17 September 1944) had the X factor! No one expected his awesome achievement when he became the

---

[23] http://en.wikipedia.org/wiki/List of mountains by elvation

first man to climb all fourteen peaks. He climbed K2 in 1979 and this was the last in his fourteen 8000er quest.

It's a long crusade for the climbers to reach all the fourteen peaks, with much work and time pressures acting as constraints. Yet, since Messner, this quest had become routine, and a Holy Grail to capable climbers. Several climbers made it. There were also women who tried but no one had yet been successful. So, the question remained: Who would be the first woman to be the fourteen 8000er?

In mountain-friendly Korea, more and more mountaineering clubs have been set up. Among them is the Gyeong Nam Mountaineering Association (Kafgyeongnam) in Gimhae. They have many active clubs in South Gyeong Sang province.

In 2006, a group of young climbers who were the next generation of the clubs under Kafgyeongnam, climbed Island Peak in Nepal. This peak was the famous lookout that offered a view of Everest. It gave the youngsters a sense of the spirit of Everest.

It was Kim Jae-Su who gave the youngsters a go at Everest. He was a devoted mountaineer and one of the directors of Kafgyeongnam. A businessman who had been managing a factory in Busan making parts for shoes, he and his wife had been successful and earned a large sum of money. But his monetary success left him less than satisfied. There was a big hole in him. In seeking a cure for his boredom, it was natural that he was inclined toward continuing his faded boyhood dream of the Himalayas. He also wrote a book titled *Spat to Everest!*, a biography based on his Himalayan mountaineering experiences.

"Let's go to Everest!"

Half-time? Or midlife crisis? That was the beginning of the fatalistic contact between Kim and the young mountaineers under Kafgyeongnam. With the money he had, Kim launched his plan for Everest and paved the way for the 2007 Gimhae Everest Expedition. His plan received wide attention and excitement not only from the young climbers but also from older folks. Their immediate enthusiasm carried over into the Everest training program. Obviously, Kim was the leader who oversaw the program.

Kim's wife was unimpressed at his overdue dream and the expedition. She had to manage the business alone and have sole care for the family during his absence. But she had reluctantly accepted it as a reality.

When the expedition news officially came out, Kim received several calls, inquiring:

"Can I join?"

One of them was Ms Go Mi-Young. Kim was impressed by Go's inquiry.

"What? The woman star climber who is working for Kolon Sport? Then, ask her to pay the price tag," said Kim.

Go was originally a sports climber whose records had gained her quite some reputation in that area. After a change of circumstances, she switched her career to the Himalayas. The transition was huge one, but she finally climbed to the top of Cho Oyu (8201m) in 2006. Everest was her second target and when she joined the 2007 Gimhae Everest Expedition at In–Chon International airport, it was the first meeting between Kim and Go, the future fourteen 8000er game players.

After a successful Everest summit, the conversation between Kim and Go narrowed into envisaging Go's next climbing plan.

"Think Big!" he said.

"Yeah, I'm sure people would be fascinated by our aim to be the first woman who reaches all fourteen 8000er peaks."

Go had successfully lured Kim. And Kim could return to his dream sport. Meanwhile, climbers could aim high with the Everest experience. A young mountaineering club calling 'Flying Jump' was born under the umbrella of Kafgyeongnam. The head of the new club was, of course, Kim Jae-Su.

In July 2007, Go and Kim successfully climbed to the top of the Broad Peak (8047m) with the backing of the Flying Jump members. In October 2007, they successfully climbed Shisapangma (8027m). On October 17, 2007, Kafgyeongnam announced to its members.

"Flying Jump is going to challenge K2 in 2008. We're recruiting young climbers for it within the Association."

It was a bold ambition, but they had someone powerful to target the young climbers. Hwang Dong-Jin of Kafgyeongnam made the announcement. He was the right hand man for Kim and Go's project. Of course, the announcement was a sensation among the aspiring young climbers in Gyeong Nam province.

'Money talks in any Big Mountain games.'—Go and Kim cunningly knew this point. Kim was a clever businessperson. Go's fourteen 8000er race was a serious business. So, whenever necessary, he invested his money into strengthening the race. Finally, they selected five junior climbers. It was Hwang who trained them for K2. Kim Seong-Sang was the bean counter.

On March 26, 2008, Kim finally became Go's manager by signing a three-year contract with Kolon Sport, the Korean sportswear giant.[24] Go, at forty-one, was set to shine with him.

---

[24] http://www.mountaintv.co.kr/board/mtnews/view.asp?tn=b_news&idx=98&page=11&search_part=&search_text=

Five

Go's grand plan in Korea to enter the women's fourteen 8000er race created a rivalry with Oh En-Sun.

At forty-two years old, Oh was a longtime Himalayan climber. She summited 8035m Gasherbrum II in 1997, Everest in 2004, and successfully summited K2 in 2007. K2 was the tipping point in her Big Mountains career. She secured a sponsorship from Black Yak and from then on chased the women's fourteen 8000er race.

Oh and Go had never met before, because they worked in different areas. Now, they were racing each other. Who would be the first fourteen 8000er woman from Korea or Asia?

In the 2008 spring season, Oh summited two mountains, Makalu (8463m) and Lhotse (8516m), with the help of Nepali Sherpas. In the meantime, Go and Kim also climbed to the top of Lhotse, the third-highest mountain in the world, also with the help of Nepali Sherpas. She had suddenly bagged five 8000 peaks.

It was cool! They could easily boost their popularity[25]. And public interest was picking up. They were the rising stars in the Himalayan mountaineering world. When Go came back home after summiting Lhotse, she courted the media:

> "While I [was] descending from the mountain, a large stone hit my hip and I had suffered for several days. I would not rush for the fourteen 8000er race. Safety is my top priority!"

Her popularity gained her a sponsor. It's a commercial world focused on money games. The Korean leisure mountaineering market has traditionally been dominated by homegrown brands such as Kolon Sport.

---

[25] http://english.chosun.com/site/data/html_dir/2009/07/13/2009071300773.html

These home brands had outgrown their market. Phase in phase out. From 1998, the pattern changed. Once top foreign brands such as North Face and Columbia entered, they aggresively stole the market. The street fashion style of people changed into cool styles and it has become common to look like a mountaineer. Kolon chased it to make the breakthrough from being export-focused and to keep its domestic market share.

Until July 2008, Oh had bagged six 8000er peaks, and Go notched up five. The difference between six and five seems minimal. However, topping K2 was going to make the difference between heaven and earth. K2 has been regarded as the hardest mountain in the women's fourteen 8000er race. If Go bagged K2, then the difference would see-saw.

True, it was still far from the leading group made up of Gerlinde Kaltenbrunner (11 peaks), Nives Meroi (10), and Edurne Pasaban (9).

But who knew? No woman in the world has climbed all the fourteen 8000er, yet. Was any Korean woman going to be the world first? Thus, Go began the 2008 season thinking:

> "By the end of this year, I'm going to climb Lhotse in the spring season, K2 at summer, and then GI and GII if I have time, and Manaslu in the autumn season."

It was an ambitious and bold plan.

Now, it was the time for Go to climb K2. Queen-maker Kim's cause had worked. The '2008 Flying Jump Korean K2 Expedition' was part of Go's fourteen 8000er race. Gyeong Nam Mountain Association had organized the expedition. And Kim, as the leader, inevitably hated losing time at any game. When they started their climb to taste K2, Kim and Go shook hands and smiled:

> "It's game on!"

Six

June 20 It was snowy during the night.[26]

June 23 It was a fine morning, but cold with temperatures below -10°C. Six Korean team climbers who slept at Advance Base Camp waited for the Serbian team climbers. When they arrived, a Serb climber said:

"It took two hours to reach ABC from K2BC."

The time had shortened considerably. At the first attempt, it took four hours because of the dangerous crevasses. The two teams started 200m of rope-fixing works above the slope and rocks. Suddenly, at an altitude of 5400m, they heard a terrifying hissing sound. It was a big rock passing by and then a stone avalanche was coming.

"Stones falling! Overhead! Stones the size of fists are falling down."

A climber put a knapsack over his head as the stones bounced over him.

The teams fixed ropes for the remaining 350m toward Camp 1. They reached the Camp 1 site at 6050m around noon, where they pitched a tent for each team.

June 24 Snow fell heavily overnight. The Serbian and Korean teams' climbers who slept at Camp 1 descended to their base camps. It felt like a homecoming. There were many conversations and laughs about the events of the day. More than anything else, fixing 1200m of rope—despite the avalanche and stone debacle—was a great achievement. And it made them much happier.

By fixing the rope to Camp 1, the climbing time shortened considerably. It would take five to seven hours of ascent. And it would take one and a half hours to descend. The fixed ropes would serve as a convenient handrail. And team members could acclimatize by climbing to Camp 1 and ferrying gear and supplies.

---

[26] www.youtube.com/watch?v=4_zCo0t4Dcc

On that day, an American-led International team arrived at K2 Base Camp. A British mountaineer originally organized the expedition.[27] But now all its members were united under the leadership of American Mike Farris. They set up their base camp at 5100m, at the highest strip in K2BC.[28]

June 25 Route works in Abruzzi slope continued in order to set up Camp 2. While high altitude porters were removing the 600m fix-ropes, Sherpas had installed 400m more ropes toward Camp 2.

From 6650m in altitude, there is a big buttress section called House's Chimney.[29] It's a 50m ice slope with an 80° wall. Climbers have to make their way between rock chasms, which needs careful climbing given the danger of stones falling.

While climbing this section, climbers can see the old ropes and steel ladder which look like a woven web. After getting through to the top, climbers have a little further to reach Camp 2 at 6700m.

The Camp 2 site at the bottom of a large boulder is the resting place on the 30° slope. The place is exposed to cold winds.

While the two team members made platforms to set up their tents, the other climbers continued to do route works with the remaining 400m of rope. Then, they went down to Advance Base Camp.

June 26 Early in the morning, Serb and Korean climbers started their climb from ABC and arrived at Camp 1 around noon. They stayed in tents for the night.

The next morning, when sun rose, some of the climbers started out toward Camp 2.[30] After climbing up House's Chimney, they barely reached Camp 2. It was cold and windy with spindrift, a windblown fine-grained snow. Their teeth were chattering and it was starting to get dark.

---

[27] http://themountaincompany.blogspot.co.nz/2008/06/good-luck-on-k2.html

[28] https://www.flickr.com/photos/25037111@N07/2642002917/in/photostream/

[29] http://k2tracks.com/home/2009/9/23/house-chimney-abruzzi-ridge-6500-meters.html

[30] www.youtube.com/watch?v=4WspcrWDV6o&index=8&list=UU2WKgh_p268Mg61-7fIaa7A

Haps and Sherpas joined their teams again. The next day they were going to climb toward Black Pyramid, fixing ropes. If they secured Camp 3, then half of the route works would be done.

So far, everything had gone to schedule. With this progress, they could set up Camp 4 on the Shoulder by July 13, and the summit push would be possible on around July 18, when the full moon was expected to appear.

Seven

Back at the Norit team, Jelle, the junior climber, had seen an unusual sight. The impression was so strong that he described it on the team's blog.

> "Jelle continues his story with some morbid details about the remains that were found by a Serbian expedition team member. He wonders if they will ever be able to identify who it was in order to notify next of kin. It seems an impossible task because they can not see anything distinct except for a mammut climbing harness."

Snow with strong winds was forecast from Saturday. In the next week, the wind speed would decrease and settle into this pattern.

Although the Norit team had no more rope until new ones arrived, just sitting and waiting was not an option. They refocused on climbing and rope reinforcement and acclimatization. Early in the morning, Team-1 members resumed their climb to Camp 2. Their plan was that, after fixing the remaining 200m rope, they would set up their tent at Camp 3, and after spending a night there, go down to K2BC the next day.

Team-2 would start their climb the next day when they received an "Okay" sign from Team-1 by radio. They worried about the risk of an avalanche, given that snow had fallen during the past few days. And then day after day, they intended to do rope fixing works continually after Team-1 had done their job.

As planned, Team-2 fixed the rope for several meters during a few hours, but it was a hard job. A blizzard was in their face at the sharp slope. The weather began to change as forecast. So they decided to climb down to K2 Base Camp.

Hugues of the French International team was climbing with his Haps on the Cesen route for team acclimatization and build-up works. He had decided to take the Cesen route, since he had climbed to 7700m through it the previous year.

Nick had stomach problems, with diarrhea. When Hugues' team was descending, he was making his way up towards Camp 1, climbing slowly alone. On reaching it, he decided to remain there for the night.

The previous year, Nick had challenged Broad Peak. He met with a disaster when a piton came away from a rock. Nick learned a valuable lesson, that he should not trust any rope since all the climbers were using that same rope. He had to carefully check its condition before using it.

On the rope, there is also beauty. Firstly, a strange feeling exists between climbers tied together by rope, like a deep friendship. And secondly, the lead climber or the last climber should not fall down. He should be ready to do the belay. There is no more famous story than Pete Schoening's belay and Art Gilkey's high drama during a 1953 American K2 Expedition, led by Dr Charles Houston.[31] Thirdly, although rope is a lifeline, climbers must not trust old ropes or ropes fixed by others.

Again, snow started to fall on the mountain. Hugues urged Nick to make a quick descent by relaying the weather forecast by satellite phone.

"Weather is worsening. Get down, immediately!"

Clouds fully covered the area around the K2 Base Camp. Snow was falling and strong winds blowing. Climbers would resume their ascent when a window in the weather opened up again.

---

[31] www.amazon.com/dp/B001B1Q7AO

Eight

June 28 It was Saturday. Wilco had wasted precious time because of the shortage of ropes. Then, he found that American Tall K2 & Broad Peak Expedition had arrived at Broad Peak Base Camp on Thursday.

June 29 With that news, Gerard and Pemba went down to Broad Peak Base Camp to see the Americans Chuck, Dave and Andy, and then to pick up some ropes. Wilco also could mobilize his team by making three party phone conferences to check the weather forecast with Abba the meteorologist, in Netherland through Maarten of Netherland Base Camp.

When he analyzed the weather information, he realized that a small window was opening in the weather for the coming weekend. "It's a crack," Wilco announced to his teammates, sharing his plan with the forecast.

In K2, it was not easy to find an opportunity for the summit push. So planning for it was always one of the difficult tasks. They needed to have five days to make a good summit plan, as follows:

> 'A day from K2BC to Camp 2, a day to Camp 3, a day to Camp 4. Then start summit push at the night and reach to the summit in the following day. Thus, a day in descending from summit to Camp 2, and then a day back to K2 Base Camp.'

But the window in the weather at this time was not sufficient to allow for a good summit push. It would mean a supporting team leaving earlier in the bad weather conditions. The summit team would descend when all the good weather had finished, and might face danger.

Norit had already fixed 3500m of rope. They needed another 400m to secure the route from above Camp 3 to Camp 4 on the Shoulder.

How would they take it? It was a serious question because he was lacking the workforce at that moment. One member still had stomachache, some were yet to acclimatize. Who would carry and fix it? For Wilco, the alternatives within his team were limited. He needed to come up with a new idea:

'Right! Use the Haps.'

Based on those assumptions, Wilco could set up his tactics as follows:

Team 1 (Supporting Team): Court, Roeland, Mark and two Haps
Start on Tuesday morning. The main task is that they climb to Camp 3, and do the route and rope fixing works toward Camp 4.

Team 2 (Summit Team): Wilco, Cas, Gerard, Pemba and Jelle
Their task is, of course, the summit push! They would start climbing on Wednesday and stay at Camp 4, and then early on Saturday morning start the summit push.
If the weather conditions were not acceptable, they would retreat to K2BC, and then try again around July 18 when the full moon was expected.

That's the Wilco's plan.
After breakfast, Wilco went the French International Camp to see Hugues, and asked him:
"We need help from your team. Can you support us by allowing Qudrat and Karim to carry and fix ropes toward Camp 4?"
But Hugues' answer was a resounding "No!" Since his team has not had enough acclimatization, the request was unacceptable to him. This was a disappointing response for Wilco.
Nick Rice was with Hugues and posted about it on his blog under the title 'Climbing Politics Take over K2 Base Camp'.[32] Politics belonged to those willing to play that game.
The next day, Nederland Base Camp also posted on their blog about what happened:

"Yesterday a discussion took place between Wilco and the Frenchman Hugues and his two High Altitude Porters. Wilco asked for the assistance from the two HAPs to fix ropes. The moment they had to make that decision the weather was very bad

---

[32] http://www.nickrice.us/index_files/k2dispatch31.htm

and a lot of snow had already accumulated. Hugues and the HAPs refused their cooperation to start today."

"Starting later was not an option for the Norit K2 team. Team 1 had to start that day to climb ahead of Team 2, who would start the following day and try to reach the summit. The window of good weather was very short. Starting later would mean the summit team could encounter problems at the end of the good weather window."

Cooperating in extreme conditions was hard. Since all their positions were different, it's understandable summit fever results.

Back on the Abruzzi route, the American International team made their first run to Advance Base Camp. Their strategy was to use the existing fixed ropes to carry their gear and supplies to upper camps and to do their acclimatization. So, Mike and Chhiring had to visit the Korean team. It's not known how the Koreans responded or how Mike obtained permission on the rope using matter. Probably, he offered some ropes to be provided later.

At this stage, Serbian team climbers were checking their oxygen masks while waiting for oxygen cylinders from Skardu.

On the same day, the Norwegian team arrived at K2 Base Camp. They pitched their tents near the Serbian team, at the center of the K2 Base Camp strip. A four-member team, three of them had attempted K2 in 2005. They had 93 days on K2, but only got a little higher than Camp 3. Based on their previous experiences, they decided not to hire high altitude porters this time. Team member Rolf Bae had not arrived yet. He was to join them a few days later.

In the meantime, Norit's countdown for their summit push had already started. They were busy preparing for their summit push. Since K2 was snowy, windy and surrounded by clouds, they checked the weather conditions with Nederland Base Camp.

Nine

July 1 Early in the morning, Team 1 members (Roeland, Mark and Court) started their climb as planned. They were carrying sleeping bags and fuel, etc. They would lodge the gear at Camp 2 and then do rope fixing works over the slope. Spindrifts were swirling in the cold air. From the afternoon onwards, the weather was forecast to improve slowly. The wind would die down, and then weather would change from Sunday. For Mark, it was day one after twelve days resting and waiting.

July 2 The summit team had started their climb. But surprisingly, they saw at the middle section of the route toward Camp 2 that Court was descending.

'Something must be wrong. What happened?'

"Roeland was poisoned by carbon monoxide," he said, urging, "Hurry up and make radio contact with Mark and Roeland at Camp 2."

Breathing in odorless carbon monoxide could happen even in a well-aired tent, while running a burner. Poisoning could be fatal in a high mountain like K2. While Roeland was cooking inside the tent with an MSR reactor[33] at Camp 2, the smell lingered in the tent and he passed out. Fortunately, Court found Roeland and Mark then pulled him out immediately. Roeland regained consciousness in a few minutes but had some complications from it.

After waiting for Team 2 members for four hours, Court suggested, "Let's go down to Base Camp!"

It was unanimous, and so the supporting team collapsed. It meant they could no longer be there for Team 2.

On the same day, at 3am, Hugues' team and Nick had woken up and eaten an early breakfast. Then, they started their climb for build-up and acclimatization works, following in the Norit members' footsteps. There

---

[33] https://www.flickr.com/photos/25037111@N07/2621839137/

was no sun, so it was a good day for the climb. Four hours later, they reached Camp 1. But, to his surprise, Nick found a climber inside the tent he had set up the last time he was there.

"Who are you?"

"I'm Hoselito."

Hoselito Bite was a Serb climber. He had applied for his K2 permit with the Norit International Expedition but had become an independent climber. Obviously, as soon as he arrived at K2 Base Camp, he had jumped onto the Cesen route for his climb.

"Yesterday I tried to climb up to Camp 2 where my tent was set up," he told Nick. "But weather was no good. So I decided to use your tent in Camp 1. I didn't touch any of your things. I swear."

After packing some necessary items, Nick and Hugues' team continued their climb toward Camp 2. Halfway up, they met Court staggering down from above. He should have been busy supporting their summit team. What happened?

Court gave them the news that Roeland was poisoned by carbon monoxide. Court himself was suffering with blisters on his foot. The problem had started when he was trekking to K2 Base Camp. Court resumed his descent, with Hugues guiding him down for a while.

When Nick arrived at Camp 2, he was glad to find that Gerard was making a platform for him. Gerard also came down from Camp 3 because of the bad weather. But Nick realized he had to share his tent with Pemba. There was no free lunch.

July 3 In the morning, Norit summit team members resumed their climb toward Camp 3. Progress was slow because of the deep snow that had been falling for the past few days. They wasted energy. When they reached Camp 3, it was 2.30pm. Their priority task was to set up the tent they had failed to erect last time. With that job done, they realized they were short of a sleeping bag. It should have been carried by the supporting team.

When tension flared with the thought of an uncomfortable sleep ahead, surprisingly a Serb climber Hoselito turned up, and said:

"I'd like to join your summit team. I'm going to try it using oxygen."

But Wilco dismissed him.

"You're not ready, not sufficiently acclimatized. We can't be responsible for any problems during your summit attempt. You shouldn't count on us!"

That seemed harsh. The rejection was a bombshell to Hoselito. There was no choice for him but to back off.

"I've got nowhere to sleep!" he said.

So a small compromise was reached. While Hoselito could set up his tent for an overnight stay, they agreed he would have to go back down the following morning.

Ten

July 4 When the summit team got up in the morning at Camp 3[34] they checked outside. The weather looked good. They started the day melting snow. They also divided the gear consisting of a 120m rope for route fixing, a 400m rope for the Bottleneck, two sets of light tents for Camp 4, a gas burner, fuel gas, groceries and other gear.

At 8.30am, they were finally ready to start toward Camp 4, shouldering gear for the climb.

Last time, Cas and Pemba put the fixed rope 200m up from Camp 3. Over there, now, a big boulder was blocking their way. Later they learned that traversing around it was the easy way. Figuring that out wasted a whole hour. The second problem was the entangled 200m rope. They had to untie it at a height with a 2.5km fall underfoot. It was a dangerous job.

"Man! This heavy load and gravity is killing me," said Cas.

Finally, over the left side, they sighted the Bottleneck serac,[35] which encouraged the team's morale.

"Let's climb hard so we can reach the Shoulder!" said Wilco.

They continued their front spiking even after the sun had set, but they realized it would take three more hours at least until they reached the Camp 4 site.

"My back is killing me," Cas said.

Jelle and Gerard were exhausted. Even Pemba looked tired. At 7500m, they faced another problem—the shortage of rope. Camp 4 was a few hundred meters away!

"Can we just keep climbing without rope?" questioned Wilco.

But they realized it was a dangerous alternative for a team that had adopted a classical siege climbing style.

"Shall we use the rope reserved for Bottleneck?" asked Wilco.

---

[34] www.youtube.com/watch?v=Dnhcf kz7WU

[35] https://www.flickr.com/photos/25037111@N07/2713149453/

But they decided not to touch it. After setting up Camp 3.5 temporarily at the top anchor, and caching 400m of 5mm rope for Bottleneck, along with Camp 4 supplies (two tents, gas, etc.), they started to run back down to Camp 3.

Meanwhile, Hugues' team and Nick had had a day's rest at Camp 2 before reaching Camp 3 after seven hours hard climbing. They all had to huddle together and sleep in a tent where there was not enough space. It was 9.45pm by the time Norit team climbers returned to Camp 3. The Haps received them with hot drinks. When Hugues heard Norit's problems and plans, he suggested:

"I can help you."

He was going to provide them with some ropes, and let Qudrat and Karim join for the remaining rope-fixing works.

July 5 The climbers in Camp 3 had an uncomfortable sleep in the small tents during the night. The overnight and morning weather was not good. They got up at 9am aching all over from the uncomfortable ground. Their minds were obsessed with getting down to base camp where warm food and comfort awaited. They collected their gear and emerged from the tents one by one.

Hugues' team and Nick wished to stay one more day in Camp 3 to acclimatize but the weather was worsening. They decided to go down. Hugues led the descent, followed by Norit members and then Karim, Qudrat and Nick.

On the way to base camp there was brief contact between the Norit and the Serbian teams. The united Serbian and Korean teams had tried to set up Camp 3 on the Abruzzi route. They talked about cooperating to climb the Bottleneck when Cesen climbers and the Abruzzi climbers were to merge at the Shoulder. The question was the Korean team's response.

In the meantime, Hugues' team had reached K2BC at 1.30pm and one more climber had joined the French International team. His name was Peter Guggemos. He had challenged K2 for the last three years in a row and was already out climbing and now at Camp 1 on the Abruzzi route.

Eleven

While the Norit team was making its summit attempt, the Abruzzi-side climbers were attempting to climb high to set up Camp 3.

July 1 Back at the Abruzzi route, American Chris Klinke (mid-thirty) and Swedish Fred Strang (31) of the American International team slept at ABC, and went back to K2BC. Finally, the team gear—4000m of rope, ice screws, snow stakes, pitons, food and the other gear—was delivered to K2 Base Camp.[36] It had been eagerly awaited.

Now, the American International team[37] could divide into A and B, so the team could carry out its plan to ferry the gear. They needed it all immediately to set up Camp 1. Among the A-team members, Chris and Fred were going to climb to Camp 1 that day.

Conditions were snowy. After breakfast, Serbian team members had visited the K2 Gilkey Memorial located at the southernmost foot of K2.[38]

July 2 Serb and Korean climbers started their climb to Camp 1 from Advance Base Camp at 6am and arrived at Camp 1 at noon. Not only were their tents covered with snow but even inside, the tents were like a powdered room. Shoveling it out took more than an hour.

Kim and Go's group was going to stay on standby at ABC. They had contacted the Sherpas' team by radio. The Sherpas were heading to Camp 2 and were intending the following day, if the weather allowed, to finish the route works to Camp 3, so Kim and Go's team could try to reach there. Camp 1 climbers would climb to Camp 2 to stock it with more supplies.

Meanwhile, Chris K and Fred of the American International team started their climb toward Camp 1. Mike Farris, Tim Horvath and Chris

---

[36] http://www.everestnews.com/pak2008/mikefarrisk07032008.htm

[37] http://goalexploration.com/s/K2.html#8

[38] www.youtube.com/watch?v=4WspcrWDV6o&index=8&list=UU2WKgh _p268Mg61-7fIaa7A

Warner went to ABC to ferry food and gear, after they sorted out the remaining cargo at K2BC.

On that day, an Italian team arrived at K2 Base Camp. Originally a four-man team, it had shrunk incredibly to two men since its other members had given up their K2 plan. Marco Confortola (37) would be one of the key players and in 2008 K2 was the leader. Roberto Manni (45) was the only team member. Before coming to K2, Marco had worked at a meteorological station on Mount Everest for fifty days. He had flown back to Milan, Italy, where he had spent a week before arriving at K2. Roberto had climbed to the top of Everest on Sunday, May 28. And then he joined Marco. They set up a large dome-shaped tent at the lowest place in the K2 Base Camp strip. Their camp was just below the Korean team.

July 3 It was a fine day but there was a strong wind. The Serbian team was going to climb up to Camp 2. A Serb teammate videoed Dren's action climbing House's Chimney. [39] Dren had a hard time climbing it because of a lack of acclimatization.

In the afternoon, Sherpas and high altitude porters tried to fix the remaining 200m rope toward Camp 3. Because of the strong wind and then the spindrift coming over the Black Pyramid, they had to retreat to Camp 2.

Kim and Go and Team 2 had stayed at ABC for two days. They then started their climb toward Camp 1, and were going to stay there. This meant putting pressure on the frontline climbers to work hard.

Meanwhile, A-team members of the American International team had climbed up to Camp 2. When the team resumed its climb toward Camp 2, Fred filmed Eric and Chhiring's actions climbing House's Chimney. This famous place was where every climber took a photograph as a souvenir. They wanted to set up a tent at Camp 2 but strong winds deterred them and, after caching their gears, they had retreated to Camp 1. Now, they descended to Advance Base Camp, where they handed over the mission to Tim and Chris W of the B-team.

July 4 The Abruzzi climbers, all the Korean team members and Sherpas were on the mountain despite the bad weather. Based at Camp 1, they had worked hard to make the big push toward Camp 3. A common goal for the

---

[39] www.youtube.com/watch?v=UJYj8_XIfiY&list=UU2WKgh_p268 Mg61-7fIaa7A&index=7

Serbs and Koreans was 'Working together' for it.[40] What else did they have in common?

By the end of the day, they wanted to reach Camp 3 through the infamous Black Pyramid. Although they tried hard their attempt failed because of strong winds. They had to get back down to the lower camps.[41]

It was around 1.30pm. Hwang, Jumic Bhote, Little Kim, Little Pasang (Pasang Lama), Tsering (Jumic's younger brother), Park and Big Pasang (Pasang Bhote) were rappelling down happily from slope to Camp 1, but Kim and Go weren't impressed. Having turned his back, Kim was just staring blankly somewhere off down the mountain. Go was standing with a tight face.

Watching this scene was painful and stressful for Hwang, who had led his team at the frontline battlefield.

Kim and Go had needed a quick delivery of the women's fourteen 8000er race. The most important element of Go's race was "speed". That Hwang's team had retreated without setting up tents at Camp 3 was a huge disappointment for Kim and Go. But K2 was such a different and difficult mountain. As it stood, the trio Hwang, Little Kim and Park had been the best among the whole Korean members.

The Italians Marco and Robert hadn't wasted time. As soon as they had set up their base camp, they had started to climb through the Abruzzi route to set up their tents at each camp. When they arrived at Camp 1, Kim and Go's team and Peter of the French International team were already there. While Marco and Roberto were busy setting up a tent at Camp 1, Eric and Chhiring of the American International team reached Camp 1 carrying their loads. The next day they were going to try to get to Camp 2.

July 5 It was a Saturday. The frontline climbers reached Camp 3 site but couldn't set up their tents. The geography at Camp 3 made it vulnerable. It had a 30° snow slope, but was a place where the wind was strong. The narrow valley between K2 and Broad Peak acted as a wind funnel, making the slopes above the camp prone to avalanches when it blew. Before retreating to Camp 2, the climbers cached their loads at the site.

Strong winds forced cancelation of the day's climbing. All Serbian team members decided to retreat[42] to K2BC while the Korean team made for Camp 1.

---

[40] www.youtube.com/watch?v=qLxTNG-XElY&index=6&list=UU2WKgh _p268Mg61-7fIaa7A

[41] www.youtube.com/watch?v=qLxTNG-XElY

Despite that, they had provided the bridge to Camp 3. It was a significant breakthrough.

---

[42] www.youtube.com/watch?v=IJ6-Xsq2Ayk&index=5&list=UU2WKgh_
p268Mg61-7fIaa7A

Twelve

July 6 Most of the Korean climbers decided to go back to base camp. They needed to recover from climbing. But Sherpas and the American team were climbing upward. While Fred was waiting for his teammate, who was on his way, Fred was resting with Little Pasang, Jumic and Big Pasang.

"Where are we?" Fred asked the Sherpas while filming.

"Oh, we are now climbing K2," Little Pasang replied cheerily.

"All right!" Fred said.

The American International team finished setting up their tent at Camp 2[43] and went inside to rest comfortably.[44] Marco's team also arrived at Camp 2 and set up their tent beside the Serbian tents.

After a chance meeting with a Serbian team member, Wilco has searched out a new strategy. When he'd faced the rope shortage problem the last time, he had made a hurried visit to the Korean team. This time he had enough time to discuss the issue with Maarten of the Netherand Base Camp so they could set up a more sophisticated strategy. And Maarten updated it with the title "Strategy Games on K2" on the team's blog.

> "As you know the Cesen route and the Abruzzi route merge on the shoulder of K2. That means that it would be possible to cooperate with teams climbing the Abruzzi. The only team high enough right now is the Korean expedition. Wilco is planning to negotiate cooperation with the Koreans. The only problem is that the Norit team only needs one weather window and Wilco thinks that the Koreans need two. The first one they still need to prepare camps and they need the second one to try to summit K2."

---

[43] http://goalexploration.com/s/K2.html#11
[44] http://goalexploration.com/s/K2.html#12

Wilco had precisely analyzed the Korean team. He had noticed it was a powerhouse.[45]

July 7 It was early evening and still raining when Marco came down from the mountain.

After having an early dinner, Marco checked the other K2BC teams' blogs. Surely, Marco with his team of only two men has desperately played his inner games with a certain outcome in mind:

"How can I set foot on the top of K2?"

He had obviously sought help from other teams to strengthen his hold on K2 climbing. In 2004, he had tried K2 without success. But he saw that K2 allowed more than 50 climbers to reach the top. The important point for the trophies was the presence of a large group of Nepali Sherpas. This season, he discovered the Korean team had four Sherpas while the Norit and American International teams had only one each.

July 8 After lunch Wilco and Gerard visited Marco. Marco was a warm man who made friends easily. He was also a good match for Gerard, who had wide friendships with other climbers at the K2 Base Camp. Wilco was more calculating, a man more focused on planning and refining tactics, and making policies. Yes, it was the right time for him to play the bigger game.

After a short meeting, Marco, Wilco, Pemba and Gerard visited the neighboring Korean team. Park and Hwang received them. Following a brief chat, they relayed a message that a cooperation meeting would take place at the Serbian team's big tent the next day. And then they shook hands like old friends. It would be a golden handshake for Wilco and Marco, but a disastrous handshake for Hwang and Park.

The Korean team invited Marco for dinner. Dining together was a common gesture for becoming friends with other teams. Late afternoon, Marco and Roberto visited the Korean camp. Everyone welcomed the duo with big warm smiles. In the kitchen tent, food was ready on the rectangular dining table. Kim sat at the furthest-inside end of the table. On his right, Shon, Park, Little Kim, Kim (Tae-Gyu) and Roberto took their seats in a row. On his left, Hwang, Go, Lee (Seung-Rok) and Marco were seated. It was a pleasant dinnertime for everyone.[46]

---

[45] https://www.flickr.com/photos/25037111@N07/2606706653/

[46] http://www.marcoconfortola.it/category/spedizioni/k2-centenario-creval-2008/page/4/ and p. 64-65, *Marco Confortola Giorni Di Ghiaccio*

Thirteen

July 9 It was a cloudy morning at K2BC. Inside the Serbian camp, Serb climbers were preparing their next carry—English air. They had checked all the oxygen apparatus. A Serb described this task:

> "Every moment we use for checking our equipment. This day is time for those things for our heads: under-caps, caps, forehead lamps, sunglasses, oxygen-masks, stop valves and bottles with oxygen. In altitude in the dark we will have not time for repairing but each error may be end for climbing."

The cooperative K2 meeting was scheduled for the afternoon. It was the main agenda of the day for the K2 Base Camp teams.

Spanish climbers arrived at K2BC from one of the Broad Peak camps. They set up their camp at a place between K2BC and Broad Peak Base Camp (BPBC). From K2BC, the distance to BPBC was about an hour, but the Spanish camp took 45 minutes. They wanted to see some friends in the French International team. One of the Spanish climbers, whose name turned out later to be Alberto Zerain (48), had brought a heavy backpack. It was an unusual move.

Around 3pm, the K2 meeting was held in the Serbian mess tent. The climbers or teams had trodden separate paths on their way to K2. But now they decided they were going to go the same way. The table was packed. At one side of the long table, three Korean members Kim Jae-Su, Shon Byung-Woo, Kim Tae-Gyu sat together.[47] Pemba took his seat next to them. On the opposite side, Gerard and Wilco of the Norit team, and Italian Marco sat together.[48] Next, the Serbs Milivoj and Iso sat together. At the end of the table were Roberto, Fred and Chhiring. Behind them, Shaheen,

---

[47] https://www.flickr.com/photos/25037111@N07/2677252037/
[48] https://www.flickr.com/photos/25037111@N07/2677251939/in/photostream/

Predrag and Dren stood. Strangely, two cooks from Serbian team attended the meeting as well. They obviously had an interest in the meeting. What for? Why?

The meeting started with warm smiles, laughs and light jokes. After a cat-and-mouse maneuver, they agreed on the general idea of 'climb together through the Bottleneck by cooperation and contributing whatever is necessary'.

But when they came to the specific issues, they realized there were big differences between the teams on their thoughts and plans. The main problem was the rope. For the Bottleneck rope, Wilco took the lead and had all the momentum. Then, Shaheen the Haps' leader in the Serbian team insisted:

"300 rope for it to make. If you want to, more 50. 400 rope, we are fixing."

"We take 400 meters. Then the Italians got 200 meters for the Traverse. So 600 meters is plenty enough," Wilco, as a motivational speaker, was persuasive.

"Maybe we need more," the Serb Iso suggested.

"We don't need more. 600 meters is plenty enough, I think," Wilco snapped.

"No, 700 would be better," Kim said.

"700? Okay, Kim says 700," Pemba responded with a smile.

Marco did not speak much English. But sitting with Wilco was enough for him to show-off. While the climbers were speaking, Gerard had the video camera rolling. The team had filmed their activities as if they were making a documentary about their entire 2008 expedition. In line with the contract with their sponsor Norit, the team also maintained a near live-blog showing images and videos to broadcast the sponsor's message. From a corner, Fred Strang of the American International team was also rolling his video camera. [49] Suddenly, the K2 climbers were actors. However, Chhiring looked bored during the meeting.

The Korean team's goal was clear. So Kim insisted that he needed 700m at least for the team's climb between Camp 4 and the summit. Notably this meant the coordination between the teams to string the fixed rope almost to the top through the whole route, and Sherpas and Haps to help lead that effort.

"There's nothing to do," an unidentified climber snapped.

---

[49] *K2 - A Cry From The Top Of The World* [DVD] [2009]

"Yeah, yeah, okay. 600 meters at the peaks. Our team's there to, uh, more..." Kim responded in that way. What did that mean?

"First, leading, second, help them, third, making the bamboo," Shaheen the Haps' leader of the Serbian team explained how to cooperate.

Pemba was rolling his thumbs and made a speech:

"...Then we're working like one team, yeah? We're working like one team. No Serbian, no Korean, no Dutch, no American. Just, there is only one Summit team... from every group."

It was a touching moment. Everyone in the tent agreed with him in unison.

"Yeah, right! We are one. Let's unite!"

Wilco had ruled K2 like a king. Now, he wanted to go a mile further.

"The question is also, who is climbing in front, you know?" He was pushy as hell.

"Two good climbers and one, two porter..." Iso finally suggested.

"Okay," someone said.

"Who carry this fixed rope," somebody asked.

"Fixed rope," someone repeated.

"The ice?" Marco questioned.

"Ice screw," Wilco said.

"Ice screw?" Marco repeated.

"These teams start one or two hours before other members from Camp 4," Iso said.

"I don't know if you're going with the summit party..." Wilco said.

Wilco had brought a handy document bag to compose a meeting memo on the points they agreed on and then got signatures from the teams. But Wilco found his memo idea was not necessary in this preliminary meeting. They might agree on nothing, except for a plan to meet again the following week. One meeting led to another.

As soon as Wilco came back to his camp, he called Marteen of NLBC with the meeting results. Marteen updated it with the title "Omhoog ?, blijven zitten?, of toch omhoog?" on the team's blog.

> "At the first sign of a good weather window the Norit team will move up again. Cooperating with the Koreans will be difficult but Wilco thinks he's got one big advantage and that's a very good and reliable weather forecast. (Words of mr. Kim the Korean Expedition leader). That information could will be the key in negotiating cooperation. Wilco also hopes the next good weather window will be around July 18th. A full moon! Wilco also thinks

this to be an advantage. For now the Norit K2 team is resting, playing chess and playing the mind game on K2."

Fourteen

July 10 It was a resting day for the Norit and Italian teams. Marco was bored and stayed outside the tent with his laptop with a porter, probably Ali. He checked all the information and tried to make a plan for his next step.

Although there was a strong wind on the high mountain, climbing in Abruzzi route continued. Korean team climbers and Sherpas and the Serbian team's Haps were working hard to ferry oxygen cylinders to the higher camps. A Serb climber wrote:

> "In the three days they intend to carry the oxygen bottles to the C4 (7.900 meters). They hoped that the weather will allow us to fulfill our intentions."

The American International team's climbers were also on the higher mountain.

A Singaporean team arrived at K2 Base Camp. Its leader was Robert Goh, with team members Edwin Siew and two Sherpa climbers. They hired three Pakistani Haps. The team was going to make their summit attempt without oxygen use.

There was a big party at lunch time. It was a feast day for Pakistani people to celebrate Imamat Day, one of the biggest public holidays. For this party, all Pakistani cooks worked together to prepare food, including desserts.

When all the dishes were delivered and displayed on the seven covered long tables in the open place in front of the Serbian mess tent, K2BC climbers and people gathered and greeted one another.

It was an unusual party for climbers. Who provided the food for this party? Did every team contribute to it? Probably not. Then, was it provided by the Serbian team? Maybe or maybe not.

For a while, the Serbian team's kitchen tent was like a butcher shop.[50] They hung the goat and yak meats on the wall. Nepalese Sherpas didn't like it since there was a cultural conflict.

Anyway, it was party time! The party started with cutting a cake. Hugues the oldest and Milivoj the Serbian team member had this honor. Some Korean climbers were there. They were Hwang, Lee (W. S) and Mrs Song. Hwang was a quiet man, perhaps because his English was limited. But it was a good time to get to know one another. Most of the Norit team members except for Mark and Roeland attended. A lunch line was forming. The Pakistani cook Nadir Ali wore the same uniform as the Serbs who were ladling the soup stew from a big soup tin.[51] Wilco and Hwang picked up buffet food and piled it on their plates. It was a great feast with delicious food.

After the lunch, there was dancing with traditional songs. Some climbers joined the group of people dancing, since it was a festival day. But most of the climbers sat on their chairs around the group, clapping their hands merrily.[52]

When Gerard got up and joined the dancing, it boosted the mood. For the last dance, the cook Nadir Ali came forward and did a solo traditional dance. He had been another dominant figure in the K2 Base Camp!

After retiring from the party, Marco and Roberto made a short visit to Norit Camp, carrying a present.[53][54] The Italians invited the Norit team members for dinner.[55]Later, Norit would invite the Italians for dinner in return.[56]

---

[50] p. 125, *strana UZENADAMBISOM:K2* by Milivoj Erdeljan, 2011 (*unpublished*)

[51] https://www.flickr.com/photos/25037111@N07/2663808512/in/ photostream/

[52] https://www.flickr.com/photos/25037111@N07/2662983297/in/ photostream/

[53] https://www.flickr.com/photos/25037111@N07/2904838555/in/ photostream/

[54] http://www.marcoconfortola.it/2008/07/

[55] http://www.creval.it/eventi2007/k2confortolaNewsletter_110708.html & https://www.flickr.com/photos/25037111@N07/2662983075/

[56] http://www.summitpost.org/base-camp-happy-memories /565477/c-565466

Fifteen

While the K2BC's party was happening, others had been climbing on the Abruzzi and the Cesen routes since that morning.

On the Abruzzi route, the Serbian team's three Haps were carrying the oxygen bottles between ABC and Camp 1. Then, a strange climber hopped onto the rope and passed the Haps' leader who was climbing at the rear of the group. He shouldered a heavy backpack. The Haps' leader asked himself:

'Who is this stranger?'

The Haps' leader couldn't figure out the stranger's identity. Most of his face was covered with a balaclava and wide goggles.

'Who is he?'

The strange climber was also curious about the Haps' leader.

'Who is he?'

He immediately sensed this man could be the key person to provide a platform for his successful K2 climb, so he snapped a shot from between his legs to figure out who the Haps' leader was.

Far ahead of them, Korean climbers were ascending toward Camp 1. Kim and Go's team had no time to enjoy the K2BC party. They had to catch-up to the Norit team so they wouldn't miss meeting at the Bottleneck. July 18 was drawing near.

Fred from the American International team was resting on a rock with the other climbers. He also had his video camera focused on climbers making their way up from below.

Before he resumed his climb, he turned his video camera around and pointed it up upwards, to shoot the other climbers ahead of him. On that day many climbers were making their ascent.

When the Haps arrived at Camp 1, they were able to check out the identity of the stranger. He was the Spaniard Alberto Zerain. And Alberto also found out the Haps' leader was Shaheen Baig.

On the Cesen route, Mark and Roeland of the Norit team had been climbing. Norit posted on their blog:

> "This weekend is a very short good weather period. Mark Sheen and Roeland van Oss decided to climb to C2. Mark is not feeling very well and has minor stomach problems. He decided to stay in C2. Roeland, just recovered from CO poisoning wants to set a personal height record and decided to climb solo to C3. He took a roll of rope with him to drop at C3 and spent the night in C3. Today both Mark and Roeland are descending to K2BC."

July 12 Early in the morning, the Italians Marco and Roberto had started their climb to reach Camp 2 within a day.

When Camp 1 climbers resumed toward Camp 2, Alberto looked very relaxed. He often handed his camera to Haps, asking them to take his picture.

The Italians met the Korean team when they reached House's Chimney. They stopped for photography and video filming sessions there.

When Marco shot some photographs of the Korean climbers, Park Kyeong-Hyo was leading the climb, while Kim was video-filming Go's action.[57]

When Alberto and Shaheen reached the base of House's Chimney, they faced an unexpected problem: a traffic jam. Kim was still filming Go's action. Kolon Sport selected it later as their commercial advertisement.[58]

Chhiring was still waiting to make his climb behind them at the base of House's Chimney. Alberto and Shaheen joined them. Alberto tried not to look at the video camera and hid his face beneath his helmet.

Eventually, they climbed to Camp 2 before sunset. Alberto must have slept that night in an empty tent. Or struck a deal with Shaheen so he could sleep in one of the Serb's tents. Was there any corruption going on between climbers? Does it common everywhere in the Himalayas?

Fred, Chris, Eric and Chhiring[59] set up two tents at Camp 2 on the Abruzzi Ridge. They needed to do this as part of acclimatization program, in order to be in a position for the summit push. They expected it at the end of the month.

---

[57] http://www.turismo.it/multimedia/art/giorni-di-ghiaccio-sul-k2-id-5948/

[58] https://www.youtube.com/watch?v=eJjs2OXlTZs

[59] http://goalexploration.com/s/K2.html#22

July 13 Sherpas and Haps climbed high to reinforce the route and carry the oxygen, despite the hurricane. The teams were desperate to stock up on supplies for the next weather window. A Serb wrote the day's blog as follows:

> "It is unbelievable—warm and sunny day here, 15°C in the shadow! But upon the mountain on over 8000m Korean Sherpa are in hurricane. The snow is over their girdles. They are trying to find right-way to BC or C4 anyhow.
> Earlier: Hurricane night is behind us. The wind has been shaking our tents all night, but we managed to keep them safe from the wind. Unfortunately, the clouds didn't rise above the top of K2, so our carriers had to get back from the C3 camp. The snow is very deep up there."

The American International team had decided to go down to Base Camp. Alberto did not have enough acclimatization for Camp 3, having woken up late in the morning. He also decided to go down. Around this time, the Norwegian Rolf Bae arrived at K2BC, at the same time his wife Cecilia was descending from the high camps.

Sixteen

July 14 It was snowing at K2 Base Camp.[60] At the top section of the mountain, a strong wind was blowing that influenced a change in the jet stream. With this weather development, hopes for the full moon on the 18th were slipping away. The weather became the main topic among the climbers, who hung out to compare weather forecasts.

All teams on the mountain had to descend to K2 Base Camp. B-team members (Mike, Chris W., and Paul Walters) of the American International team decided to go down to K2BC after spending two nights at Camp 1 and two nights at Camp 2.

Wilco, Pemba and Gerard returned from their Gasherbrum base camp trek.

Late in the afternoon, another K2 meeting was held in the Serbian mess tent. Who attended the meeting? It's hard to be precise but Mike, the leader of the American International team, also mentioned it in his blog. And a Serb also posted rough notes about the meeting.

> "...in our tent was meeting of leaders of all expeditions in K2BC. There were Dutch, Singaporean, American, Italian and Korean. We made agreement for collective upsurge to the top. The biggest problem is Betelnik, ice-rock which is about 100 m high. We will put the rope on it all together. Few next days there are expecting bad weather. When the forecast be good we will meet in C3 and start to K2 from there. It needs to install more 300–700 fix-ropes."

Due to the nature of live reports from K2 Base Camp, it was easy even for climbers on nearby mountains to get the necessary information about the K2 climb. They could easily gather information about their tactics and

---

[60] www.youtube.com/watch?v=UJokY1xE_Ak&index=4&list=UU2WKgh
_p268Mg61-7fIaa7A

the next climbing schedules. It was just a matter of Internet surfing, so could a motto have been set up?

'When they go, I go.'

Of course, this piggybacking happens in every Himalaya mountain climb nowadays. Some climbers deliberately arrive late at base camp with their fingers crossed:

'Somebody might have already done the notorious rope works.'

They hope to jump-start their acclimatization by taking advantage of the logistics put in place by earlier expeditions as soon as they arrived at base camp.

In this way, K2 has gradually become crowded. The big question on this one, and a problem raised by the teams that arrived earlier was:

"How do we climb the Bottleneck given the anticipated congestion?"

Meanwhile, the three French climbers on K2 posted an unexpected statement:

Statement from Yannick, Christian, and Patrick (French)

"We would like to clarify a misunderstanding. We have indeed acclimatized on the slopes of Broad Peak but not above 6500 meters."

Did they break a common law by trying for Broad Peak? Surely, the statement clearly says so.

Free-riding was a frustrating issue for Broad Peak climbers. Since accidents occurred all too often, the Broad Peak climbers might be fed up with such piggyback riders. If they remained silent on the issue, they surely knew the problem would escalate. More climbers from the surrounding mountains would come so it was a recipe for disaster.

Broad Peak climbers had to get tougher about defending themselves. Silence or ignorance was not the solution.

July 15 Around 6am, a sudden, loud sound came from the mountain. Loose and broken ice-rock had started falling from a big serac around 7000m in altitude beside the Cesen route. Climbers who got out of their tents could see a huge avalanche coming down from the mountain onto Godwin-Austen glacier and then rolling continuously toward the flank-side of Broad Peak.[61] It was ominous but a spectacular moment. All the cameras were madly clicking and video rolled to film the event.

"What a morning!"

Since these kinds of events have been a routine for K2 climbers, climbing on the Abruzzi route continued.

Chris and Eric of the American International team decided to stop over for a night at Camp 1, and then resume their climb to Camp 2 the next morning. Their key goal in reaching Camp 3 was to set up a tent there.

On their way up to Camp 1, they met Peter Guggemos who had spent three days at Camp 2 despite the poor weather conditions. He had decided to head back down to K2BC.

Back at K2BC, Marco declared with his national flag:

"K2 is my mountain!"

K2 was the Italian mountain. The Italian legacy was on the line for Marco and he didn't need to worry about anything for the coming climb. The cooperation meeting had boosted his morale. Having only a two-person team was great. This time, his victory was surely guaranteed.

A group of Korean climbers were cutting bamboo with knives[62] and saw Marco hoist his flag up high.

They were going to use the bamboo to make markers with red tape attached. These red markers would help to find their way on the featureless snow slopes above Camp 3, where they were going to head as soon as the weather improved. Sherpas were working hard to ferry oxygen bottles to the camp for them.

---

[61] www.youtube.com/watch?v=ZlyQZh6veLo

[62] http://blog.daum.net/_blog/ArticleCateList.do?blogid=0Xolp&
CATEGORYID=2

Seventeen

July 16 A Serb wrote of their team's activities that day as follows:

> "There are no clouds over top of K2. Early in the morning we were starting to C2. At first we will poke the snow around our tents in C1 and then in C2. We will sleep there.
> Our tents are OK and all of equipment is OK too.
> Some minutes after high-noon clouds are on the sky again. The wind is stronger. Leader of our expedition Mico Jovovic arrived from Serbia this morning in BC."

Climbers had had a disappointing weather forecast. The weather window would not open until early August.

Court Haegens of the Norit team had decided to go home. He had never recovered from his painful foot blister, and it eventually led him to quit. It was an invisible loss for the Norit team.

After breakfast, Court said goodbye to the team.[63] Gerard updated his blog with a title "Morale hit a new low for the team". Wilco had been dealing with the loss.

At 3pm, the third K2BC meeting was held at the usual place, the Serbian mess tent. Those climbers able to be identified from photos and footage are:

> **Right side**: Mike, Chris W., Paul, Kim, Shon, Pemba, Gerard[64]
> **Left side**: Milivoj, Miodrag, Serbian team's liaison officer Sabir Ali, Wilco, Marco
> **One End**: Roberto, Serbian team's cook Nadir Ali Shar, and so on.

---

[63] https://www.flickr.com/photos/25037111@N07/2673427635/in/photostream/

[64] *The Summit*, a documentary film by Nick Ryan

It was interesting that the Serbian team's liaison officer attended the meeting and sat at the center of the table. Why would a non-climber like a liaison officer show up at the team's strategic meeting? What for?

Sat cosily next to the liaison officer was Wilco. Helluva, the liaison officer, was leading the meeting and he was making a trail-party list.

Why? Were there any conflicts of interest between the teams? Did Wilco use him for this reason?

After a lengthy debate, the teams wrote down the names of the lead climbers on a piece of paper.

> Hwang, Park, Jumic, Pasang—Korean team
> Shaheen—Serbian team
> Ali—Italian team
> Pemba—Norit team
> Chhiring—American International team
> Karim (Qudrat—*erased*)—French team's Hap.

The Serbian team just one? The Norit team only one, as well? Why not an equal contribution?

And who was Ali from the Italian team? Wasn't he a mere porter? They included Chhiring temporarily. Mike, the leader of the American International team, was not sure of the contribution. Qudrat was included, but Hugues the team leader didn't attend the meeting, and he was replaced by Karim. How did this mass confusion arise?

Next, they intended deciding on the gear each team would contribute but having spent too much time already, they agreed to resolve the issue at the "Leading team" meeting. It was set for three days' time, July 19 at the Korean camp.

Since the Serbian team leader was there, Milivoj could sign an interim agreement. Under their signatures was the date: July 16.[65] They also agreed the next K2BC meeting would be held when the weather window opened.

---

[65] p. 171, *strana UZENADAMBISOM:K2* by Milivoj Erdeljan, 2011 (*unpublished*)

Eighteen

July 17 It was a calm and beautiful morning at Camp 2 on the Abruzzi route. The climbers decided to make a challenge for Camp 3. Reaching camp 3 was difficult and would take seven to eight hours. In the Korean team, Sherpas were to carry the oxygen cylinders to Camp 3. When the first group of Sherpas departed, the American International team climbers also started out.[66]

When Chris and Fred were climbing the Black Pyramid, two Sherpas were below them, shouldering oxygen cylinders. The Sherpas were using the familiar Nepalese Sherpa head-strap,[67] made of a band that extends under the entire pack and over their heads, spreading the pressure points from the shoulders to the head.

When Chris, Fred and then Eric reached Camp 3 site (7400m), they exchanged their delight. The high scenery had changed and they could also inspect the steep China-side of the mountain. Chhiring was busy making the platform and setting up a tent.

Rolf and Cecilia of the Norwegian team were also arriving. Everyone was happy to set up their foothold on Camp 3. Fred also filmed the climbers' exchange.

"Finally here. Such a relief," Fred said.

"Fantastic job," Rolf responded shaking hands with Fred.[68]

"Good job," Fred agreed.

"When you go up your muscles tell you, you have to breathe now," Cecilia said.

---

[66] http://www.steamboattoday.com/news/2008/aug/08/resident_recalls_k2_tragedy_claimed_11_lives/ & http://goalexploration.com/s/K2.html#15

[67] p. 128-129, *K2 - Pa Liv Och Dod* by Fredrik Strang och Per Johnsson

[68] http://www.businessinsider.com.au/the-summit-2008-k2-tragedy-2013-10#this-is-where-many-of-the-details-get-sketchy-according-to-confortola-he-and-mcdonnell-began-descending-on-saturday-morning-but-stopped-to-help-three-stranded-members-from-the-korean-team-41

It was a gorgeous day. The climbers could see the route for Camp 4.[69] They had spectacular views of Karakorum and the China side, and even deep into Tibet over the Windy Gap and Sky Kangri.

Did Alberto the Spaniard climb to Camp 3 on this day? Most likely! Alberto left a few photographs. In one of them Eric was climbing the Black Pyramid.[70] Another one was of Alberto at the Camp 3. It was not selfie. Someone took it for him the next morning.[71] Alberto looked tired. He might have lain squeezed into a tent at Camp 3 alongside three Haps.

What was the response from the other teams about this kind of piggybacking?

Mike Farris, the leader of the American International team, didn't stay quiet about the matter. He was clearly irritated by these climbers and commented about it in his blog on July 18. He didn't name them, but he clearly mentioned, "there are few." Climbing is a small world so they knew who they were.

On the same day, the Singaporean team had climbed to Camp 2 with great difficulty. They had been struggling with acclimatization and team work. Team leader Robert wrote of the events:

> "On 16 July 2008, the 3 HAP went up to C1 and slept there for the night. The next day, Mr Zulfiqar and Mr Jhan Baig complained of loss of appetite and headaches—symptoms of Acute Mountain Sickness (AMS). Mr Mehraban had a headache and was given a pill for it. Mr Zulfiqar returned to base camp after 30 minutes of climbing towards to camp 2. Mr Mehraban and Mr Jhan and the team continued to camp 2 (6700m). Robert and Edwin, Kami and Jamling had to share Mr Zulfiqar's load as well as lighten Mr Jhan's load because of his AMS. All HAPs returned to BC that same day while all our members stayed in C2..."

On the Cesen route, Hugues' team continued climbing toward Camp 3, while Nick decided to go down to K2BC from Camp 2.

---

[69] http://goalexploration.com/s/K2.html#17

[70] Image Name: Alberto Zerain-02-Del C2 al C3 en el K2, The image was removed

[71] http://desnivel.com/expediciones/alberto-zerain-ante-la-arista-mazeno-del-nanga-parbat

At K2BC, the Norit team's summit members decided to resume their climb, after having had a long break. Gerard was going to climb to Camp 2 a day ahead, and Wilco, Cas, Jelle and Pemba were going to climb toward Camp 3 the next day.

They had a small window of opportunity and their plan to reach Camp 4 was unrealistic, as Maarten of NLBC summarized:

> "Their goal is straightforward and simple. Start climbing to C3 and sleep overnight. If the weather holds, climb towards camp 3.5, the stack of gear just below the shoulder of K2. Pick up the gear and try to establish C4 on the shoulder. Afterwards descend immediately to K2BC. The weather will worsen again during the beginning of next week."

Meanwhile, Tim from the American International team decided to go home to attend to family matters.[72] He left with Kirsty (who trekked to Base Camp with British-born Australian Paul Walters) and Taimur, the team's liaison officer who escorted them down.

Hugues and his team had reached Camp 3. But the afternoon weather forecast did not look good so they decided to go all the way down to K2BC immediately.

A new team of climbers had arrived at K2 Base Camp. Romanian-born American George Dijmarescu was leading this team, which consisted of two Sherpas and two Romanian clients.

George's team had difficulties climbing Everest through the Tibet side because the Tibetan situation was boiling over with the forthcoming Beijing Olympic Games. So they diverted their plan to K2.

If everything went well, it would be the first summit by a commercial expedition. It was another ambitious K2 challenge.

---

[72] http://thealtitudeexperience.com/blog/tag/k2/page/2/

Nineteen

July 18 Nothing happened on this day because the full moon remained shouded in clouds. Instead, all the climbers in Camp 3 on the Abruzzi route had to go down to K2BC because of the dismal and snowy weather on the mountain. A grim weather forecast came out from the Pakistani Meteorology Agency:

'Monsoon is coming!'

They expected this weather pattern. There has sometimes been flooding around the Indus River after heavy rain. Although the weather would not affect the Karakorum, the weather window would not be open until the end of July because of the surrounding unstable conditions.

Norit climbers were on the mountain. From early in the morning, four members had started making their way towards Camp 3.[73] But Gerard who had stayed a night at Camp 2 chose the safe side. His was a life of creeping fear since he couldn't trust the weather conditions. It would be better to descend, have some rest and then wait for the next weather window rather than going for the push in the new snow.

In the outside world people would be enjoying the hot summer. But the K2 climbers were stuck in wintry conditions. Some climbers started to say:

"I want to go home!"

A long, dismal weather pattern hit the climbers hard. It was difficult being away from home for such a long time but most of the climbers were still passionate about their jobs.

Meanwhile, the Korean team members visited Gilkey Memorial at the southernmost foot of K2—a memorial for climbers who lost their lives on the mountain. [74] There were many plates attached to a rock

---

[73] http://vimeo.com/1400671

[74] http://blog.daum.net/_blog/ArticleCateList.do?blogid=0Xolp&
CATEGORYID=2

commemorating the dead. It was a timely visit for Korean team climbers, but they couldn't hide a rising tide of pessimism.

"Somebody among us can die like them."

Nick had been seriously considering switching his climb to Broad Peak. He probably had a Broad Peak permit. When he heard the news that eight climbers had reached the summit of Broad Peak, he planned with Hugues to visit the Italian camp in Broad Peak and, if possible, visit the Spanish camp as well to get some information and talk about team works. When they arrived there, Hugues received a call from home in France. He had to go back to K2 Base Camp.

July 19 Norit climbers had to go down to K2BC. Marco was watching them through his binoculars. When they reached the glacier, Marco ran to welcome them warmly.[75]

The climbers struggled hard to take their next steps on the mountain. But now they were stuck in K2 Base Camp a Singaporean climber wrote:

> "We stayed C2 on 17 and 18 and return to BC on 19 July 2008. The HAPs suffering from AMS made no effort to further acclimatize upon their return to BC."

A Serb climber reported:

> "The team is back at BC, as there's no let up in the weather. Although snowfall is light, it is continuous, weighing down their tents and covering the ground with half a meter of snow. Plus it's cloudy."

Waiting games in the bad weather had been hard for the team so although they had decided to stay in K2BC they began climbing again.

Because of the unforseen overstay, first, they had to extend their visa period until the middle of August and change their flight schedules through their travel agencies.

Second, they had to survive with the remaining food they had since they were scraping the bottom of some of the food barrels. They needed to reorganize their supplies of food by either reducing their intake or finding

---

[75] http://www.marcoconfortola.it/2008/07/page/2/

replacements. Some teams bought yak from the local seller who brought it to the mountain and killed it.

According to the memo from the previous meeting, K2 Base Camp climbers should have had a meeting of the leading climbers in the Korean camp, to talk about the gear each team would contribute. But there is no information about it. Maybe they canceled the meeting for some reason.

On that day, Tall K2 & Broad Peak team members came to K2BC to have a look at the climbing conditions for their future challenge.[76]

July 20 Hugues' news from home forced him to decide go back home. Qudrat's K2 contract period with him was also expiring. Qudrat was supposed to leave K2BC soon to join a Korean Expedition. He was pre-contracted to guide for the expedition's challenge on an unclimbed 6000m peak in Shimshal, around the first of August. It was a strange double contract.

Anyway, Hugues sent his travel agency a request for porters so he could get out of K2BC on July 22. His tents and equipment were on the high camps but he didn't care and was going to give them up regardless. With this decision, his Hap Karim's climb was also over.

There were many colorful flags flapping in the strong wind at K2BC.[77][78] But the morale of K2BC was dropping sharply and climbing became a rare event. Snow and avalanches had kept climbers on edge. They were running out of patience as well. But it was all about coping with pressure. They came here and they existed to climb to the top of K2.

They played more cards and board games.[79] Some climbers came out of their tents to rearrange stones or their platform with shovels to make it balanced. The Serbian team wrote:

> "Clouds, snow, wind . . . Every day in BC is the same. And the sun? Only seldom peeps behind the clouds. All of us are nervous. All the days we are in our tents. We go out only for snow-clearance."

---

[76] http://www.k2tallmountain.com/blog/K2_Tall_Mountain/Welcome.html

[77] https://www.flickr.com/photos/25037111@N07/2554371014/in/photostream/

[78] https://www.flickr.com/photos/25037111@N07/2606706885/in/photostream/

[79] http://vimeo.com/1399512

Twenty

July 21 There was a surprising claim:

"I climbed beyond Camp 4 on the Abruzzi route!"

His name was Jorge Egocheaga, a Spaniard. But there was some doubt about his feat because even Sherpas who had worked hard couldn't reach Camp 4 because of the bad weather. In the 2009 K2 season, Jorge also claimed that he summited to the top of K2, which no one had summited then. Seeing his summit photograph as evidence, other climbers including Fred Strang at K2BC doubted his claim. Then, Jorge insisted that he stopped 10m before the summit. Just 10m short! His reason was that it was too dangerous to go further in the severe weather.

When the Pakistani authorities who kept the official summit record rejected his claim, he responded that he was happy to regard his feat as a personal achievement.

Norit climbers had a day for cleaning up around the K2BC. Then, news came the leader of Singapore team had sacked Jehan. The team was in trouble with the angry high altitude porters in the Serbian team who confronted the team about its decision. The liaison officer of Serbian team even jumped into the debate. Was that right?

Something strange might have been going on in the Serbian camp. There were many signs that its Haps were acting as freely as they liked. This raises some questions:

"Who was leading the team?"

"Who hired whom?"

"Who was the real leader?"

The team seemed like it had two leaders. So, were the Serbs in a state of confusion? Was the team dominated by a Pakistani force? The power of high-altitude porters and Pakistani kitchen staff was strong. There was someone behind them—an important person invisible to others. In order to understand the background of the 2008 K2 climb we have to uncover this person...

Qudrat had a plan to bring back their gear from Camp 3 on the Cesen route. He planned to go up with Karim but he realized two men weren't enough to bring all of the heavy load down. It was a long way up and down. So, Shaheen of the Serbian team joined the mission.

Then came the good news. Finally, the weather window was to open! K2BC climbers were shocked when they received new weather forecasts predicting four fine days from July 29. These four days would be enough for the summit push and to reach the top.

The forecasts gave a huge boost to the climbers' morale. Suddenly all the frustration dissolved as new energy and high spirits kicked in again. The waiting was over!

However, it was not the most impressive news for the outgoing climbers, especially Hugues. He had already told his family and friends several times, "My K2 is finished. I'm going home!" He had just been waiting for porters who were on the way.

But with this favorable weather forecast a doubt lingered in the back of his mind.

"I've also waited for this chance for a long time."

He was at a crossroads in choosing 'Home or K2'. It was easy to read Hugues' mind in such a mood.

"Stay at K2BC," said Gerard.

"If you put things off for 2–3 weeks, you might be on the top of K2," said Wilco, also.

The temptation was strong.

"I have no problem since my gear is loaded high on Camp 3," Hugues may have said. "But if this good weather is delayed, I'll have no choice but to go to Skardu."

With this compromise, his plan to automatically go home was demolished.

During the afternoon, the Korean team had a group photography session. It was part of their media publicity in support of the Korean teams participating in the 2008 Beijing Olympic Games. The Summer Olympic Games were ready to start. While all team members and Sherpas were gathering outside the team's mess tent, Kim waited for Go outside her tent. When he slid inside, she was standing in front of the mirror with her make-up on. Kim filmed her actions with his video camera.

They finally joined their teammates and they all stood holding a long banner: "Fighting for Korean Players at 2008 Beijing Olympic! From all the members of Kolon Challenge team K2 Expedition."[80]

There were almost twenty people including the team's liaison officer, two kitchen-hands and two Pakistani helpers. They shouted at the tops of their voices.

"Fighting!"

That evening, like at BPBC, a party was to be held at the Serbian soup tent, which had been transformed by porters into a music room. There was a rumor there would be a disco party that night. After dinner, porters burst into songs of joy together. Hugues, Karim and Nick joined the party along with the Norit climbers.[81]

However, a disco was just a rumor. While Karim and Nick also sang a song, everyone clapped their hands. Gerard was a talented cultural ambassador. Cas took an empty food drum, and beat on it vigorously with his palms to boost the mood.

"Dung Dung, Dung Dung Dung!"[82]

---

[80] http://foreigntravel.tistory.com/m/post/1424

[81] http://pakistank2.blogspot.co.nz/2008/07/tout-tait-organis-pour-mon-dpart-du.html

[82] https://www.flickr.com/photos/25037111@N07/2694237092/in/photostream/

Twenty-one

July 22 As usual, the mountain was covered in clouds. Climbers spent time together to allay their boredom.

The waiting was tormenting for the climbers and, partially out of a mixture of eagerness and boredom, Serb climbers tried to ascend to Camp 1 to acclimatize. But the bad weather on the mountain forced them back to K2BC.[83]

Someone interpreted the unstable weather as being influenced by the sun-moon eclipse happening around that time. It was a compelling explanation at first, but the climbers soon accepted it as one of many arguments which had no basis.

As Qudrat had to leave K2 soon, Hugues couldn't allow an opportunity to pass. He had to find a replacement for his coming summit push so he hired Jehan Baig as his Hap, the high altitude porter sacked by the Singapore team.

Around that time, another rumor mushroomed that Marco was going to switch his climbing route from Abruzzi to Cesen. Why did he entertain such an idea despite already having set up his high camps on the Abruzzi route?

In the late afternoon, the climbers scheduled a meeting at the Serbian mess tent so they could discuss tactics for the summit bid. At the previous meeting, they had decided the next one would be held when the weather window was open.

Before it started, Marco decided to visit the Korean camp to meet the team leader Kim. When he got to the Korean big tent, however, he found that Kim and Shon were both napping.[84] Marco took a photograph of them asleep before he went away.

---

[83] www.youtube.com/watch?NR=1&feature=endscreen&v=Azz6u7QOMIE
[84] p. 64-65, *Marco Confortola Giorni Di Ghiaccio*

The crowd at the Serbian mess tent was larger this time. Hugues was in attendance, and this was his first involvement in the K2BC meetings. That meant most of the teams in K2BC—Norit, Italian, Korean, Serb, French, American and Singaporean—attended.

Two teams were conspicuous by their absence. The Norwegian team didn't turn up. Their interests were still different. They wanted to climb independently. Maybe, contributing gear didn't make sense to them. George's team also didn't attend. His team wasn't ready and he was already fed up with these kinds of Base Camp meetings in Nepal.

All seats at the table were taken. Many climbers had to stand to watch the meeting. Everyone wanted to challenge K2. Serbian team members had big expectations of the meeting. They showed it by wearing custom-made outer uniforms. Interestingly, the team's cook Nadir Ali Shar also wore it. He stood just behind Sabir Ali Changazi, the team's liaison officer.

Why would the cooks turn up to the teams' strategic meetings, again? Just for fun? Was there any purpose? Was there any peer pressure on the meeting's result from them or any Pakistani group? If yes, why? Anyway, it was the Serbian mess tent.

They needed to review or renew matters from the previous meeting. The exact content of the packed meeting was not clear. But, George wrote about it in his blog. His understanding of the role of the leading climbers was:

> "The selected climbers—consisting of mainly Nepali Sherpa, Korean Sherpa, Pemba from the Norit Team, and Dorje one of the Sherpa guiding a Western climber—will join forces with three Pakistani climbers to forge ahead, perhaps an hour or more hour before everybody else starts. It is said that one or two Korean members will join forces with the Sherpa and Pakistani to fix about 500–600m of rope at the Bottle Neck and perhaps a little below it. Then the plan is that most members will follow to the summit."

The next important topic was 'securing a definite date to go for the high camps'. Norit team suggested July 29, while the Korean team wanted July 30. Hugues just sat there like an observer. He was not sure about these suggestions and decided to speak out:

"We should wait until July 25. Fixing the date now is useless because of the unstable K2 weather," he said.

All agreed on Hugues' suggestion, and they decided to hold off on the matter until the July 25 meeting.

The last thing to do was to 'wrap-up' the meeting, for the team leaders to put their signatures on the paper.

While each leader was signing his name, most of the climbers in the tent were watching with delight but some had a vague look in their eyes. Climbers who had their cameras didn't lose the chance to take some shots of this moment. Gerard was a video-man, and again he was filming the scene at the corner table.

Serbian team leader Miodrag didn't sign on the paper. Instead, team member Milivoj signed. Why?

When Kim was about to sign, Shon helped him to handle the papers. Shon's main role was communication, so his priority was attending all the K2BC meetings rather than climbing. He was a shrewd strategist. Maybe, the Serb Milivoj has been acting in a similar role for the Serbian team.

When Kim signed at the bottom of the sheet, there was a climber who couldn't hide a tiny grin. Shaheen, the Serbian team's Hap, was sitting with Hugues and Mike Farris at a corner table. [85]

To him, Kim's signature had a million-dollar value. Shaheen had bragged about himself as being a 2004 K2 summiteer. Most of the K2BC climbers took him at his word. His achievement in 2004 had come not only from his own climbing technique but also the power of the Sherpas. The K2 50 anniversary team hired them. At this 2008 season, the Korean team had more than enough Sherpas.

But, some climbers were skeptical about the ceremony. They had some questions in mind.

'What's the meaning of this signing? Are we going to bag K2 summit by words or politics?'

'The summit would be achievable by climbing skill and hard work only. Why was this signature or cooperation necessary? Can we get to the top of K2 by combining our forces with weak teams?'

They knew that, sometimes, the wrong union with the largest ego, pretending and seeking a false reputation, could kill climbers on these kinds of big mountain games.

Some climbers felt the K2BC meetings or any agreement were merely social engineering. But that was the way things went.

---

[85] www.youtube.com/watch?v=SsKgBbDztSo&list=UU2WKgh_p268Mg 61-7fIaa7A

The meeting was adjourned until July 25.
The Norit team updated its blog about the meeting.

> "One thing is for sure. All signals in the weather model predict a good weather window starting from next week Monday. The Norit K2 team, together with the Italians (Marco Confortola) will start their ascend (Cesen route) on Tuesday July 29th. Together with the Korean Expedition who will start one day in advance on the Abruzzi route. They will meet where the Cesen and Abruzzi routes merge on the shoulder of K2."

Strangely, the points were not about the meeting results, but that the team was looking forward to the weather forecast and the possible climbing dates.

Twenty-two

July 23 Early in the morning, Hugue's guide Qudrat Ali had to leave K2BC. He was heading down to Skardu with Meheban, a Hap who came from Shimshal to go with him. It was a snowy morning.

His teammates Hugues, Karim, Jehan, Nick and his friends Sabir Ali, Shaheen, Little Hussein, Cook Nadir came out to say goodbye. Gerard also emerged to shake hands with Qudrat.[86]

It was another boring day for K2BC climbers but state of mind was everything. Eating well, reading books and listening to music on their iPods were the order of the day, as a Serbian team member described it:

> "In BC K2 everything is OK but the weather. It is snowing again. We are healthy and full of energy and enthusiasm."

Around this time, the Norwegians put a body into a crevasse near the base of the Cesan route.

At K2BC, Cecilia held out her hands to Rolf when pop music *Sail away with me, honey* rang out.

"Let's change the mood!"

They danced together joyfully. Cecilia was leading and she was a good dancer. A member of Tall & Broad Peak came to K2 Base Camp for a hike. They'd also been waiting for the weather to challenge Broad Peak.

For all the climbers, waiting for good weather for the summit push was boring, especially during the night. They watched repeat movies on their tiny laptop screens.

July 24 In the morning, the three French climbers left K2BC. And Oh from the French Broad Peak International expedition came to K2BC to visit the K2 French International team.

---

[86] http://pakistank2.blogspot.co.nz/2008/07/cb_23.html

K2 climbers sat outside. They were all fed up with the boredom of the waiting games. Sat in the sunshine, they read and re-read letters from their families and friends. Doing handwashing became a routine job at K2BC.

However, summiting K2 or climbing K2 was the highlight of a climber's career. They analyzed the newly arrived weather forecast. The summit push day was delayed 24 hours because of the wind speed. They hoped for no more change. Anyway, a green light was coming.

A journalist for the Discovery Channel came over to K2BC to film, and interviewed Wilco.[87] Wilco was going to shine as a K2 star. After the interview, Wilco told Maarten of NLBC, and he updated the Norit blog with a title "Nothing to tell..., but great expectations!"

> "No News because all expeditions are waiting for the good weather window. Wilco was interviewed for the Discovery Channel and tomorrow is THE BIG MEETING. All expeditions will attend and the final decisions will be made about the summit push next week. The Norit K2 expedition is already longer than 2 months in K2BC. For the last period of three weeks they have been waiting for the weather to improve. Tomorrow we will publish the final outcome from the big meeting."

---

[87] https://www.flickr.com/photos/25037111@N07/2698839908/in/photostream/

Twenty-three

July 25 The Serbian team updated their blog as follows:

> "Expeditions of French and Spain abandoned BC K2 yesterday. We are looking at the sky and wait for window opening. Upon on Abruci Rock all is ready for the final ascent: ropes are fixed, advantage camps are installed, oxygen is there. After 10 days sun punched the clouds for first time."

It was another cleaning day for the Norit team. Cleaning was the part of the campaign under the banner 'Respect the Mountains'.[88] Marco and Roberto joined Norit members and went up to Advance Base Camp on the Abruzzi route and collected about 75kg of garbage.[89]

After lunch, the Spaniard Alberto came to K2 Base Camp with his two teammates. They visited the French-led International team for tea. When they were about to leave to return to their Broad Peak base camp, Gerard came and sought a solution for a problem he was having with his computer.

Around 3pm, the Spaniards returned to their base camp. The K2BC climbers gathered and greeted one another in the Serbian team's mess tent for the final K2BC meeting. The mess tent soon became crowded with climbers chatting. It was a real melting pot of languages. The meeting was the final call 'all for one, or one for all'. They couldn't miss it.

This time, Rolf and Lars from the Norwegian team also attended. Since the team's choices had shrunk dramatically, they had to take part.

---

[88] https://www.flickr.com/photos/25037111@N07/2541616582/

[89] https://www.flickr.com/photos/25037111@N07/2700623005/in/photostream/

Cameramen, including the Discovery Channel, were happy to roll their cameras for this significant meeting. If we check out the photographs, the climbers in attendance were:[90]

> (**Seated** from the right end) Kim, Go, Shon, Wilco, Rolf, Lars, Marco, Roberto and Gerard (filming).
> (**Left**) Miodrag, Hugues, Milivoj, Iso, the Serbian team's liaison officer Sabir Ali, Mike, Chris W.
> (**Standing** from the left) Eric, Karim, Pemba, Chhiring, A Discovery Channel photographer, Predrag (filming).
> (**Standing behind**) The Serbian team's cook Nadir Ali, Jehan, Shaheen, Little Hussein.

There were high expectations of the meeting. They reviewed the weather forecast to make sure of their summit-push plan. The most important point of the meeting was fixing a D–day for the joint effort from Camp 4. The Korean team insisted the starting day from Camp 4 be the night of July 31 and summit day August 1. But the prevailing opinion was 'Start July 30 and summit July 31'. They didn't want to lose even one day among the possible climbing dates.

Then, they agreed on the gear each would contribute. The total rope would be 600–800m. This was made up of 400m from the Norit team, 200m from the Italian team and 200m (reserve) from the Korean team. They would carry another 200m, if possible. In this way, they built a winning tactic.

But there were doubts: Will they take all the ropes and gear responsibly? What would the climbing be like? No one could predict it. They had no choice but to firmly believe in the power of one.

After the meeting, the teams hopped outside to have a group photograph session. The Discovery Channel photographer was already waiting for them with his camera equipment set up. Wilco and Shaheen were the main channel of communication in organizing the meetings. They posed in the center of the front row, and other climbers surrounded them (*see* p. 117).

> **Standing** in the front row: Kim Jae-Su (L), (Kneeling in the front row) Hwang Dong-Jin, Go Mi-Young, Karim Meherban, Shaheen

---

[90] http://www.explorersweb.com/polar/news.php?id=17440

Baig, Wilco Van Rooijen (L), Little Hussein, Jehan Baig, the Serbian team's assistant cook Nisar.
Middle from the left: Robert Goh (L), Dren Mandic, Eric Meyer, Chhiring Dorje, Chris Warner, Mike Farris (L), Milivoj Erdeljan, Miodrag Jovovic (L), the Serbian team's liaison officer Captain Sabir Ali, Muhammad Khan.
Back row: Shon Byung-Woo, Hugues d'Aubarede, Pemba Gyalje, Marco Confortola (L), Roberto Manni, Predrag Zagorac, Iso Planic, Rolf Bae, Lars Flato Nessa.

The whole Serbian team was out there, including the liaison officer and cooks. In another group picture Shaheen Baig was replaced by his team's cook Nadir Ali Shar. The cook posed with Wilco while the other 26 climbers surrounded them.[91]

These were odd photos taken in the 2008 K2 season. Was there an undetected bold and ambitious scheme being cooked up by the Serbian team? Specifically speaking, by Pakistani staff?

It was possible that someone might have set up a Pakistani Haps-cook in the Serbian team. It could be a secret experiment to copy the structure as happens nowadays with the Sherpa-cook working company in the Nepalese climbing world. Thus, what was good for the Pakistani group was good for the Serbian team. Success would be good for both parties. But it was a risky scheme, too. If it failed, the results would affect to Serbian team as well.

The real person behind the scheme was probably Nazir Sabir who was not only the head of Nazir Sabir Expeditions[92] but also the president of the Alpine Club of Pakistan. Nazir Sabir Expeditions organized the 2008 Serbian K2 Expedition. For the scheme, Nazir ambitiously hired the Shimshal veterans—Shaheen, Little Hussein (Muhammad Hussein)[93] and Muhammad, and the cooks including Nadir Ali Shar.

With this investment in the project, he hoped the expedition's success was not only his future but also the pride of Shimshal, his home village.

---

[91] http://abcnews.go.com/Nightline/photos/climbers-fall-death-attempting
-k2-11361962/image-11362174

[92] http://nazirsabir.com/news/nse_brochure%20final.pdf

[93] http://www.everestnews.com/pak2008/sunny07252008.htm

All the climbers were on edge throughout the meetings. Just like the Abruzzi climbers, the weakness in the Cesen climbers was also the summit pyramid, which was greatly unknown.

No one had seriously climbed the summit pyramid section yet. So, Wilco and Hugues were going to be heavily dependent on Shaheen, who claimed he could easily find the route. They had high expectations of him, as if he were the real leader of the leading climbers.

So, Hugues, Marco, Roberto and Wilco had to take memorable photos with Shaheen. Then, Go posed for the Discovery Channel.

After a series of group photos, the teams broke up and headed back to their own camps. The strategic meeting was over. Who would reach the summit? Only the best would. At K2 Base Camp, they wouldn't know any difference.

Maarten of NLBC posted on the Norit blog the results of the meeting under the title "The Big Meeting":

> "The Koreans will start on Sunday 27th of July. They will climb the Abruzzi route and need to start earlier because they still have to build an entire camp 3.
>
> On Monday the Norit K2 team and the Italians will start their ascent. Their goal for Monday is to reach C2. Tuesday July 29th they will proceed to C3. The next day Wednesday they first have to climb to the improvised C3.5 and pick up the materials they left there. That same day they have to fix ropes towards the shoulder of K2 and pitch C4. C4 is just a small camp and it's only used for eating, drinking and get some rest.
>
> The next morning Thursday 31st of July very early in the morning (around 01.00 hr.) they will start the final Summit Push."

Twenty-four

So, the countdown to the summit push had already started. If we consider the summit push day as July 31, the final meeting day on July 25 was D–6.

July 26, D–5
With freezing winds gusting 18–30 km/h, it was a big chill day, remarked by everyone.

"Brrrr . . . "

"Yes, very cold."

"You've put enough clothes on."

"But it's not warm enough."

"My tent is damp. Condensation."

But all they wanted was to reach the summit. Before getting into their pole positions, they geared up for the summit push by sharpening their weapons, such as the dull crampons, and charging their batteries.

Some climbers left their last thoughts on blogs. Mike Farris wrote on EverestNews.com:

> "Dear EverestNews, The first major summit push on K2 is scheduled to start tomorrow, with the lead teams hoping to summit on July 31. Other waves will follow if the promised weather window holds true. Most of the teams on the Abruzzi and SSE Spur are working together to fix the route.
> There has been little activity on the mountain in the last 10 days due to winds on the upper peak. Mike"

The Singaporean team also updated their plan on EverestNews.com:

> "Just when patience is running thin, there is a crack in the awful weather. Most of the teams at base camp are starting their summit bid on Sunday. Our guys are waiting for them to get higher up to

avoid the jam on the mountain and will head for Camp 1 on
Tuesday. That's when the wind is expected to be milder."
"The windows at K2 are extremely narrow," Robert said. "They
appear and then disappear in three or four days."
"Fingers crossed that this window will let them get up to Camp 4
to complete their acclimatization."

Nick Rice who wrote a daily dispatch posted:

"Hopefully, the next dispatch I will write will detail our summit
day. Wish us luck!"

Hugues also wrote what was on his mind in his blog:

"I wish everyone could contemplate this ocean of mountains and
glaciers . . . The night will be long but beautiful."

Gerard wrote:

"Sin e anois a oharide. Ta an t-a af teacht."
(That's it for now my friends. The time has come.)

Seeing it, the Irish newspaper *The Sunday Times* reported on July 27,
2008 that "Gerard McDonnell attempts to become first Irishman to conquer
K2".

Twenty-five

July 27, D–4

Let the battle begin. Early in the morning, the air was crisp and invigorating. From the grid, most of the Abruzzi teams were moving busily up the mountain. Abruzzi and Cesen were going to merge like a zip at the Shoulder. "Set Up Camp 4!" was the first goal. Since nobody had been to Camp 4 so far, they knew there were risks. The biggest questions were:

"Are we still up for the K2 match?"

"Do we have enough acclimatization for the summit push?"

"Who will make it to the top of K2?"

They'd worried their acclimatization had weakened during the bad weather days. But now it was time to get on the waves of a climb. If they didn't, they would lose the possible summit opportunity.

The Korean and Serbian teams' climbers left first in a solemn mood but they were still encouraging one another:

"Good luck, and return alive!"

They'd lived with the dream. Now, it was time to set off and achieve it. Their goal of the day was to reach Camp 1.

Since Camp 1 was a small space, it wouldn't hold all the climbers. The Norwegian team was a dark horse. They had left for Advance Base Camp one day early. It was a flying start for them but a risky decision to start in the strong wind conditions. Today, they were supposed to move up to Camp 2.

The American International team intended to go as high as possible to see whether they might be in a position to go for the summit. The team decided to climb up the mountain in two parts.[94]

---

[94] http://www.everestnews.com/pak2008/mikefarrisk07282008.htm

Team 1—Fredrick, Chhiring, Chris K., and Eric would leave for Camp 1. They would start a bit late to avoid the crowds.

Team 2—Chris W., Paul, and Mike would follow along two days later with the other teams' Team 2 climbers. Team 2 climbers from the Korean and Singaporean teams were going to leave for Camp 1 on July 29.

Marco changed his mind since he had never tried the Cesen route before, and decided to adhere to the Abruzzi route. Thus, Italian team had to leave directly for Camp 2 on July 28. George's team decided not to participate because his Romanian clients were not ready due to lack of acclimatization.

Deep snow piled up on the slopes. When the Korean and Serbian climbers reached Camp 1, they were surprised that most of their tents were buried by the storms. A Serb climber reported:

> "Our tent is destroyed but equipment is OK. We will sleep in Singaporean tent."

July 28, D–3
Around 5.30am, Norit team climbers started toward Camp 2 through the Cesen route. Roeland was to stay at K2BC until the next day when he was going to climb to Camp 2 with Mark Sheen to carry out a mission: pack a tent and bring it back to K2 Base Camp.

Serbian independent climber Hoselito joined the first wave. Two Austrians—Christian Stangl and Thomas Strausz Mag—had also planned to join the wave but withdrew without explanation. Like Hoselito, the Austrian duo had gained their K2 permit via the Norit International Expedition. But the tactics employed by the Austrian duo during their climb were unknown.

Hugues with his two Haps and Nick also started their climb in the morning. They noticed that Gerard was split from his team and was climbing alone. What had happened? Had he quarrelled with Wilco over some climbing issues? Since the quarrel, Gerard couldn't make his mind up whether he would start with the main group or with Mark. But he decided not to lose his summit opportunity.[95]

---

[95] http://www.nickrice.us/index_files/k2dispatch59.htm

About the same time, the Abruzzi climbers were moving toward Camp 2. Strong winds whipped up spindrifts which almost blinded their faces. They arrived at Camp 2 after House's Chimney and found their tents had semi-collapsed and were covered by heaps of snow. Even within the tents there was powdered snow. They also found the Norwegian climbers were still there. They were supposed to have gone toward Camp 3 but the strong wind had blocked them. More and more climbers arrived until Camp 2 was packed with so many they had to all squeeze uncomfortably in the tents together.

Meantime, most of the Team 2 climbers checked into Camp 1.

According to the forecast the weather was set to improve. But no! The wild north-west wind was sweeping across the K2 slope. The cold from the driving wind was pinning the climbers down.

Twenty-six

July 29, D–2

"Wind, wild winds!"

"Amazing weather, eh?"

"Yeah—Crazy!"

The K2 weather was unpredictable and it was worsening. In these strong wind conditions, climbing the infamous Black Pyramid would be suicidal. So the Abruzzi climbers decided to stay at Camp 2 for another day, and radiophoned their decision to the Norit team on the Cesen route.

Wilco decided to wait until noon for the Abruzzi climbers. Then, if the wind died down, all the climbers on both routes would climb. But Hugues, along with two high altitude porters, had already left for Camp 3.

Later, Nick joined Hugues and told him of Wilco's calculated decision. The weather had worsened. However, Hugues planned to climb to around 7500m the next day to set up Camp 3.5. Hugues knew the topography well since he had climbed this area the year before; also he was a fast climber so it was unlikely he would meet the younger waves of climbers on the mountain.

Meanwhile, the climbing didn't go as planned. Some climbers started to show physical problems, caused by sudden climbing after long breaks. Among the worst affected was Shaheen, the Serbs' high altitude porter. He'd been fit and healthy until that morning. But now he could neither eat nor drink. He was able to take medicine, and received emergency treatment but was already exhausted with High Altitude Cerebral Edema (HACE) or High Altitude Pulmonary Edema (HAPE). He had vomited several times during the night. The Serbian team reported the mishap through EverestNews.com:

> "One advantage-carrier was sick in C2. He was disgorging and we are not sure if it was blood or not. He was laying down helpless. An American doctor got him an injection and we got him some

medications. He was better in few minutes and spent the night at C2."

Eventually, the Serbian team decided to let him descend the following morning. They radio-contacted K2 Base Camp so someone could climb up to help his descent. It was obviously the starting point of the fallout of the team's summit push. This fallout would affect not only the team but also the entire squad of teams, since Shaheen would not be able to help the climbers in the Bottleneck.

Everyone regarded him as the best in the leading team on the Bottleneck. He was going to carry the 30m rope for the Traverse. So, this fallout was not a good sign.

Meantime, Team 2 climbers heard the news about the summit teams' delay and problems, so they also had to return to Camp 1.

July 30, D–2
Because of a day's delay, the summit assault was changed to August 1. So, July 30 fell victim to D–2, again. It was a fine day, but there were still strong winds. The Abruzzi climbers started toward Camp 3 through Black Pyramid. The team had left Shaheen behind because the help from K2 Base Camp was still on its way. Since strong winds were blowing, their hands were too cold to operate the jumar clips. Then, once they started to meet the ice-rocks of 90m and 20m at the 7000m altitude, it took a long time for each individual climber to advance.

When they arrived at Camp 3, they were lucky they could re-erect the tents they had set up 20 days previously. They had also to erect several additional tents.

On the same day came the news that Broad Peak climbers including Oh, the Korean woman, had summited the peak.

When the Serbian climbers checked into Camp 3 they found another huge problem. A team member explained it, later.

> "On the arrival to C3 we discovered that the two departed porters forgot the food in C2 and that we would be in the mountains without food during the following days. Still we succeeded to find some sweets and soup in our rucksacks and to borrow some food from other expeditions.

Until the end and the descent we did not have anything to choose but we were not very hungry."[96]

Of course, the Norit climbers had headed toward Camp 3. Easy-going Mark had joined the team at Camp 2 for a while but to his disappointment he had to stay behind again since there would be no space in higher camps.

By the time the Norit teammates arrived at Camp 3 (7050 m), fierce weather was on the way.

> **Wilco**: "Any comments?"
> **Cas**: "None. Bloody sport. No. it's a superb day. Damn, you don't get many like these. I'm surprised the French have left already. That's favorable."
> **Wilco**: "Yes."[97]

By then the Frenchman Hugues was arriving at Camp 3.5 with his Haps and the American Nick. Anytime, their tents could blow out. There was a gale-force wind and once again the unpredictable weather of K2 threatened. Doubt swirled around. Wilco shot more footage of that moment.

> **Wilco**: "It's July 31 (*in fact, it was July 30*) 5.15pm. The wind hasn't really subsided yet. We're even lucky that the tent is still up and in one piece.
> We're lying here with our shoes on and backpacks ready in case the tent rips. I think this is the moment when our expedition ends. It was all in or nothing. We ended up in this storm. And we'll have to wait and see if no other expedition members are in trouble."

Around 1am, the weather turned deadly, delivering weather bombs and strikes. How terrifying! Hoselito the Serb had to abandon his gear and tent when the violence escalated. And the blow forced the tentless Hoselito to share with one of the Norits. Wilco shot the incident while Cas tried to make a commentary:

> **Cas**: "If Carlos says there was no wind . . . The Serb's tent has collapsed. The Serb is in our tent now. I saw his coat blowing past

---

[96] p 2, *2008 K2 Serbian Report* by Milivoj Erdeljan the team member.
[97] www.youtube.com/watch?v=zCY1w4JbE9M

us outside. We have to wait and see whether we can help the French. If not, then it's time to get the hell out of here."

Twenty-seven

July 31, D–1
By 8am the Norit team members were still not sure how the day's weather would pan out. But as it was so far a fine day they decided to trust the weather forecast.[98]

Before resuming their climb, Wilco recorded his prospects in a tiny camcorder.

> **Wilco**: "We had a bizarre night. There's almost no wind and we need to fix the ropes in the final stretch . . . So we can set up Camp 4 in a moment."

But their hesitation meant they were running late.[99]

Meanwhile, Hugues' team at Camp 3.5 had climbed toward Camp 4 site. Finishing the last rope work, they finally reached the Shoulder and then the 7700m mark. The Camp 4 site looked good. Broad Peak and Chogolisa were looming brilliantly. The team immediately started to chop and dig ledges out of the slope to set up the last camp.

Back on the Abruzzi route, the hurricane wind had also battered the climbers during the night. They barely had any sleep but in the morning, they were happy to find the wind had gone. Fine weather had finally arrived.

From Camp 3, it would take 6–8 hours to get to Camp 4 through the real Abruzzi route.

Here is the deep snowfield section, a precipice and a continuous slope-wall section. The most dangerous part in the section is the large serac

---

[98] https://www.flickr.com/photos/25037111@N07/2579686837/in/ photostream/
[99] https://www.flickr.com/photos/25037111@N07/2715969791/in/ photostream/

measuring a 45° slope near the Shoulder, because if the serac should collapse an avalanche would occur. Climbers have to pass this area as quickly as possible wearing a light backpack, making sure to mark the way with flags but without the need to fix ropes.

Little Pasang—the Korean team's Sherpa and also the lead climber—was the best choice to plough the snowfield partly because he was in the best condition. The snowfield was knee deep. As the lead climber, he had to push up one step widely to plough the snow.

Later, a funny story was playing out behind him. More than ten climbers shouldering tents and gear were following him, but at the same time holding a rope! The climbers who were dependent on a guide rail were relaxed. We have never before seen such a spectacular climbing scene involving a rope within the Camp 3 - Camp 4 section.

Perhaps they were simply considering safety first? If someone lost balance then he or she could easily fall from the precipitous slope.

In front of Go, Hwang was wearing Kolon's down suit and was guiding her. Kim was climbing close behind. That was the typical climbing format for Go's fourteen 8000er race.

Time went fast. It was already 1.21pm and they were at 7520m when the Abruzzi climbers stopped to rest. They needed to change the leading role. At last, Marco took the lead. On such a deep snow slope, it was a relief to see Jumic helping him by doing some trail-breaking.

At the 7650m mark there was a 3m high overhanging serac. Once they made it over this they were to get their first glimpse of the upper summit pyramid.

Forging ahead, Marco, Jumic and Little Pasang arrived at Camp 4 around 3pm. Marco greeted Hugues, who had already set his tent. When the Korean Sherpas were preparing their team's platforms with snow shovels, Kim arrived. And then, Hwang and Go roped together. Kim took some video footage on Go's arrival at Camp 4 site and also some still photographs.[100]

Then, the Serbian team arrived.

Since they had a big event ahead of them, the climbers had no time to lose. It was wrong to waste too much time on making platforms when they needed to sleep.

---

[100] http://www.kolonsport.com/komiyoung/date/photo05/pop_
photo10.html

However, the Serb climbers were just wasting their time, simply watching while the other teams worked. Something must be wrong with them. Other climbers sensed the Serbian team's lethargy. It was something to do with Camp 4.

Marco also became bored waiting for his teammates and decided to move on.

"Let me put the bamboo flags over there!"

He took some bamboo markers and climbed toward the higher Shoulder.[101]

Later, Roberto arrived. But Amin didn't. Why? What had happened to him?

After 4pm, Pemba arrived too. He was the first of the Norit climbers to make it to Camp 4. His climb had taken nine hours. It was already late in the afternoon so he had to dig a platform with his shovel as fast as he could. After a while Wilco arrived and started to record himself with his tiny camcorder.

> **Wilco**: "We're arrived at Camp 4. It's 4.30pm. We're here with the Italians, Koreans and Serbs. Tomorrow we'll see whether we can make a start."

And then, Jelle of the Norit team arrived at Camp 4. He would join the Italian team in their tent. This was a deal made at K2 Base Camp between Wilco and Marco since Wilco had already calculated there would not be enough space for Jelle in Norit's tents. When Wilco saw Gerard and Cas arriving he started to film them.

"How are you feeling?" Wilco asked.

Gerard, wearing sunglasses and his mustache frosted by cold, was almost in tears.

"Ah, so happy to be here... I could almost cry... '06, I failed to get here. That was great... All six get here. Here we are now and it's wonderful... So..., okay guys. It's a beautiful climb. This is already something yeah... yeah."

Cas arrived behind Gerard. He tapped Gerard's shoulder while passing, and joined his team. Wilco was also proud of the achievement. He took some selfies.

---

[101] p. 64-65, *Marco Confortola Giorni Di Ghiaccio*

The sun was already going down over the west side of the K2 summit pyramid. When Marco returned, he was not happy with Roberto. He realized that something was wrong. But what was it? Whatever, they had to hurry to finish making their platform.

Chhiring arrived at Camp 4. He was the first of the American International team.

All teams were busy excavating the icy slope to make the platforms for their tents. While Chhiring was working hard setting up the tent site[102], Fred and Eric arrived.

"I'm very cold," said Eric.

Winds were mild but it was certainly getting brisk. Eric immediately covered his face with his Cold Avenger mask. Fred looked up at the mountain and started filming the events at Camp 4 with his video camera:

"Tomorrow is gonna to be a very tough day. The Bottleneck looks scary and shit!"

Kim was also video-filming Go's work. Hwang and Jumic, Go and Little Pasang were assembling the two tents in pairs.

Alongside, the Serbian climbers were smiling and watching with interest as Kim filmed Go.

Fred continued rolling his video camera. Then he crossed to Kim and asked teasingly, "Mr. Chairman! How do you feel? Good?"

"Yeah, Good!" Kim answered, giving Fred the thumbs up.

---

[102] https://www.youtube.com/watch?v=FHYX_6VS17w

Twenty-eight

A Serb climber, Predrag, approached Fred.

"How are you feeling?" Fred asked.

"Good! It's better than I expected," he answered.

Nearby, Marco was crouching down taking pictures of Broad Peak. So, Fred approached to him to film.

"How do you feel?" Fred asked.

"Ciao! I laid down... flags over there," Marco said, pointing in the direction.

"Very good!" Fred said.

Until then, the four Serb climbers had done nothing. They were simply preserving their space next to the Korean team. Muhammad, the high altitude porter, strayed away moving towards Camp 3. He had been eagerly awaiting his companions. What was wrong with the team? Why were they just hanging around the Korean team, doing nothing, as if their only hope lay in the Korean team? Had something messed up? Perhaps they had brought oxygen bottles but no snow shovels, which were essential to dig spots for their platforms and tent work! Had they even brought tents? Muhammad, waiting for Little Hussein and Milivoj, kept asking himself the question:

'Will they bring a shovel?'

It was taking far too long. Alternatively, they could simply wait until the Korean team finished their platform works and then borrow their shovel. It was embarrassing and frustrating for them. They were tired of waiting, crouched around the Korean team's tent work. Many climbers had still cameras and video cameras. But how about ropes and gear? Did they have enough ropes and ice-screws? Finally, a Serb climber was able to borrow a shovel. Teammates helped by kicking away the lumps of cut snow, but Muhammad was still off awaiting his teammates.

For climbers, what has to happen immediately afer setting up tents is to melt the snow. They must make drinking water. At this altitude, when climbers are moving, they breathe quickly and heavily. Lungs work desperately, transporting the oxygen that is being supplied to the red cells to the brain. Therefore, climbers need to drink water. While making water, other climbers were gazing at a precipice gully under a huge overhanging serac. It was the Bottleneck.

The usual Bottleneck scaremongering was going on between the climbers.

"How can I climb over there?"

None sounded confident.

The job was to climb all the way up the Shoulder and then Bottleneck gully after reaching its base. The gully, covered with iced snow, looked hard enough but then they would climb onto the top of the Bottleneck at a 50° angle. From there, they would need to negotiate the slippery passageway connection to the lower steep section of the Traverse. This section is known as the crux among cruxes. It was formed with a rocky band-like slab and the ice and rock remain severely exposed on its surface. The summit was over the Traverse and the snowfield but it was not yet visible from Camp 4 (*see* p. 119).

K2 is surely a 'mountaineer's mountain' and many have called it so. To climb the Bottleneck and beyond, the K2 climbers had to ensure that nothing was taken for granted. But had the climbers forged at Camp 4 the expertise to tackle potential problems? No one seemed sure exactly what to do, particularly knowing that the experienced Shaheen had dropped out at Camp 2. Although some climbers had been exposed to problems and learned from them, there was no communication between the teams in Camp 4. It was strange. On top of that, the shortage of rope had been looming but had had largely been covered up. Most of the climbers were not yet aware of it.

Back in the Korean team, Little Kim and Park, who were transporting the oxygen bottles, still hadn't reached Camp 4. It would soon be dark. So Jumic and Little Pasang set off down to help them. Finally, Milivoj and Little Hussein arrived at Camp 4 to join their Serbian team. Chris K also arrived at Camp 4 as the last member of the American International team,[103] and then, finally, Little Kim and Park with Jumic and Little Pasang.

Over twenty climbers had by then checked in at Camp 4. However, they couldn't figure out the exact number since one team was still missing: the Norwegians. There were all set to join the summit party so why were they so late? When the Spaniard climber, Alberto, arrived at Camp 3 in the

---

[103] http://goalexploration.com/s/K2.html#24

afternoon the Norwegians Rolf Bae, Cecilia Skog, Øystein Stangeland and Lars Nessa were still there but were about to resume their push up.[104]

When the Norwegian team left for Camp 4, the Korean Team 2 climbers arrived at Camp 3 in Abruzzi. The Singaporeans and an American International team member were intending to check in as well. Since Alberto had experienced no company for days among the emptiness of K2, he felt as if he was losing the ability to speak. He had eagerly awaited radio contact with his Broad Peak teammate Aitor. At 5pm, Alberto made the call. There was no reply. Alberto thought his radio battery had gone flat but actually, at that particular time, his friends were busy pushing toward the Broad Peak summit.

The Norwegian climbers arrived at Camp 4 at dusk, around 7.30pm. They had to work hard to set up their two tents before darkness fell across Camp 4. The Serbian team set up a tent. But how many would sleep in it? Six climbers in a tent? Many Camp 4 climbers were already exhausted because of the late arrivals. The hours drifted by, with just four hours remaining till midnight. Sleep loss occurring at this altitude would be one of their common problems. It would bring physical and mental fatigue to them all.

Finally, D–day was coming. They had paid their dues for everything that K2 wanted of them. After grabbing a few hours' sleep, they would get up to start their climb toward the summit.

---

[104] http://www.dagbladet.no/2009/09/30/nyheter/innenriks/ulykke/ k2_and_mountain/8351263/

Twenty-nine

August 1, D–day

At Camp 4 alarms beeped. It was 10pm, time for the leading climbers to gather for the ascent.

The climbers had to get up. But nobody was outside. At 11pm, they started getting into their gear but nobody came out to lead. Since Shaheen had dropped out at Camp 2, there was clearly a leadership vacuum.

But if they wanted to go for the summit, they had to carry out the plan. Someone needed to take ACTION.

However, it was an almost absurd demand at this altitude. Then, someone called to the leading climbers from outside:

"Guys, come out!"

It was Pemba, who had taken care of the matter. He called loudly. Again and again he called. But no one showed and he was simply wasting precious time.

It was also the time when climbers realized the risky life of politics. Marco had failed to arrange his Hap as his tribute. His Hap Amin dropped out before Camp 3. Marco slowly realized the result—lack of gear including rope would make for a high-risk situation. But maybe the error would turn out to be the path to his success? Although the climbers realized there were some problems, what could they do about them at this complicated stage? The K2 Bottleneck and beyond held them under pressure. So, in their small tents they were merely repeating their rituals for their summit push. The routines were: snapping on their headlamp; putting on the down suit; zipping up; melting the ice-snow to make water to fill their flask; checking gear and backpack; putting on boots; attaching a spiked crampon to each boot and so on.

Yes, D–day had come. They'd all lived with the K2 dream, prepared to risk everything and here was the moment. Eventually, Hwang the Korean climber came out. He was quiet. And then Jumic and Little Pasang joined them.

Around that time, Alberto reached Camp 4 and met the climbers. Alberto was a surprise visitor who appeared to come from nowhere. The climbers couldn't recognize him since his face was protected by the cover. And there was no moon.

"Who are you?" Pemba asked the stranger.

"My name is Alberto Zerain, a Spanish climber. I'd like to summit K2," Alberto introduced himself.

Alberto? The lead team members responded quickly. Most of them had never heard the name before, let alone spoken with him. But in the dark, minus 20 degrees, the climbers were not in a position to reject him. Unstoppable now, they simply ignored him.

Pemba called out more climbers. Chhiring joined the team. And then, Little Hussein. All were Nepali and Pakistani climbers except for a lone Korean climber, and there was not a single climber from the Serbs and Western climbers! It was worrying to realize the climb would be heavily dependent on Sherpas and high altitude porters.

Alberto had no idea what to do. He had no place to rest and his patience was wearing thin. He just stood there with nowhere to go. With only an ice axe and no workforce for rope-fixing in the Bottleneck, Alberto positioned himself as a flanker.

The leading team set out at 1.30am. It was three-and-half hours behind the original schedule. In the pitch dark, they started to head toward the middle of the Shoulder where the ice slope was. This would eventually join the Bottleneck base.

Little Hussein knew the route and led the team. Jumic, Little Pasang and Pemba were in the front group, then Chhiring and Hwang. Six in all. Alberto followed them.

Meanwhile, the climbers at Camp 4 had planned to start their climb an hour after the lead team. As soon as they joined up with the lead team, they planned to climb the Bottleneck and the Traverse as quickly as possible. But, some climbers were already experiencing high-altitude sickness. Among them, Jehan Baig, Hugues' Hap, could not continue because of a crushing headache that wouldn't shift. He had complained of altitude sickness since Camp 3.5. Hugues thought it was AMS (cerebral edema) and gave him medicines. His altitude symptoms returned at Camp 4. It took him a very long time to turn on his headlamp, and strapping his crampon took 30 minutes. Karim had to help him. Waiting for him was one of the biggest disappointments for Hugues. He had wished to start earlier than the other climbers. And outside he worried about his feet because of the possibility of frostbite in the freezing temperatures.

In the Netherlands, Maarten of NLBC had already started his live-feed coverage on the Norit climbers' ascent so Wilco was kept busy communicating with Maarten, sometimes via Roeland at K2 Base Camp.[105] Although it was 2.30am, no team in Camp 4 had started the climb. Had the Korean team received the "not ready" message from the leading group via radio?

At around 2.50am the Norwegian team was the first to begin the climb. Around 3.10am, the Korean team decided to start their climb anyway. And then Hugues' team and the Norit team followed them, and around 3.40am, along with Marco and the Serbian team. It was no surprise why the Italian and Serbian teams started their climb so late.

"Oh my goodness, I spilled water!"

This was tech-savvy Nick. He was melting the water in his small tent but he overturned the tin and the water spilled into his socks. Though it would be a minor mistake in daily life it should not happen at Camp 4. A small mistake could prove to be a big one at this altitude. Sometimes, it could ruin the whole plan. One small mistake could mean the end.

Some climbers, especially the American International team members, hadn't made up their minds whether to go for it or not.

The main party climbers were still climbing the Shoulder. There was no moon, but the starry host of stars and constellations made a stunning display. When they had climbed a distance of 350m from Camp 4, they found an unexpected length of rope.

'Eh! Rope laid here on this easy slope of the Shoulder?'

Was this the reason the leading climbers stopped often and were still climbing the Shoulder? They didn't advance any further. The main party of climbers was getting closer to them, in fact they were just 20–30m behind.

"Do they have a shortage of rope?" said Kim.

"What? Their rope has finished? That's hard to believe," responded Go.

But that was the reality. That they could go neither up nor down but merely stand still was deeply upsetting. It turned out the early rope-fixing on the easy part of the Shoulder had caused the problem.

After making calculations, it transpired the total rope was only 500m. 100m short! Marco should have known this problem earlier when he met

---

[105] https://www.flickr.com/photos/25037111@N07/2720128455/in/ photostream/

Roberto at Camp 4. Yet they hadn't informed anyone. Marco was still behind the other teams. He didn't hurry. And Roberto had quit his climb.

Thirty

Climbers stood still along the Shoulder. All the plans for the day's climb lay shattered on the steadily rising Shoulder.[106] Since the plan to send up a lead team ahead had not worked, their high hopes were all but dead. Someone in the lead group should go down to cut the ropes and fix the problem. Amid the darkness and chaos, the Korean team's sirdar, Jumic, made a decision.

"I'll run down to cut the rope and bring it up."

Chhiring and Karim decided to go down and help him.

"My feet are freezing," said Jelly.

The main party of climbers was left with nothing to do. Some started to take flash photographs of their teammates[107] but the fact was, in the predawn darkness, just standing on the middle of the Shoulder was too cold.

About 4.45am, dawn broke over K2, and before 5.15am they could see the boundary between light and darkness across the horizon.[108]

"No way, I can't climb anymore!" said Jelle.

He made up his mind to turn back. The rope problems at this dizzy altitude and the long wait in sub-zero temperatures were two of many reasons for him to decide not to go any further.

For the first time they could also see a few leading climbers up ahead. They were far below the Bottleneck base. A line of the main group of climbers was also visible around them—Lars and Cecilia, the Norwegian climbers with a stranger, and the Korean climbers, Hugues' team and the Norit team. They were dependent on ice axes because they didn't need to clip with the rope laid on the slope.

---

[106] *See* p. 116 in this book.

[107] https://www.flickr.com/photos/25037111@N07/2904775807/in/photostream/

[108] https://www.flickr.com/photos/25037111@N07/2905620150/in/photostream/

The morning weather looked near perfect, with only a slight layer of cloud visible to the north-east over China. They hoped it was merely morning mist and would disappear. They could also see the last group of climbers coming up from far below. This comprised Marco, the Serbian team climbers and the American International team climbers.[109]

Thankfully, rope was on its way up. Jumic was behind the Serbian team. He had worked hard to cut the ropes. Now he resumed his climb in order to pass the rope to the front group.

After overrunning the Serbian team climbers and Marco, Jumic stopped and signaled something with his hand. But Marco was not moving. He had stopped to catch his breath. He bent down on one knee and leant on his ski poles. The temperature was still sub-zero.

By now the sky was dawning in the east. Light splashed golden fire across the peaks.

"It's a cracker!" The Norwegian Lars, who hadn't been higher than 6200m, couldn't miss this golden opportunity.

"I'll take a shot for you," he said.

When he captured Cecilia, she was looking back to check Rolf's movement below her. Little Kim, wearing a Kolon down suit, was in the photo as well. He was dwarfed and his face was covered by sunglasses and an oxygen mask.[110]

Alberto, who squeezed into the leading group, was also exposed by the daylight. While waiting for the rope, he too took selfies with Broad Peak in the background.[111] The Korean climbers—Hwang, Park, Go and Kim—resumed their climb as the ropes were gradually passed to them.[112]

It was past 6.10am. Fred and Eric had stopped their climb far below in the mid Shoulder, and they looked up. They could see Chris who had decided to catch up to the lines of slow-paced climbers. And they could see a tightly spaced group of climbers moving unhurriedly.

Sitting together in the morning sunshine, Fred and Eric expressed doubts about their climb. They had invested money, years of planning,

---

[109] https://www.flickr.com/photos/25037111@N07/4427221410/in/ photostream/

[110] http://www.bbc.co.uk/worldservice/programmes/2010/08/100803_ cecilieskog.shtml

[111] http://www.blogseitb.com/vitoriagasteiz/tag/alberto-zerain/

[112] htt https://www.flickr.com/photos/25037111@N07/4427223252/in/ photostream/

training and climbing, but their climb was over now. Fred recorded it with his video camera and said:

"7900m. Disappointing day. Total miscommunication because of gear who... will bring it... and we are way back in time. We're really late. I don't know what the fuck we're gonna do."

Eric also said:

"Very disappointing."

When daylight fully dawned, Fred and Eric turned around. It was about 7.30am.[113]

---

[113] *See* p. 116 in this book.

Thirty-one

Now, all the remaining climbers entered the Death Zone. Lars took a shot toward Rolf below. Tired looking, Rolf managed to smile broadly. Little Kim, Cas, Dren, Iso, the Serbian team climbers and Chris were climbing behind him. The climbers were following the leading group, some of whom had reached the Bottleneck base. It was 8am when the Korean climbers and Hugues eventually joined the lead climbers. When Pemba and the Korean team arrived at the Bottleneck base, the rope problem was fixed. And they could immediately begin their climb into the Bottleneck gully.

Breathing heavily, Jumic had transported the salvaged ropes. When he reached the bottom tip of an outcrop of rocks in the Bottleneck, he decided to take a break. When Jumic saw his teammates who were climbing in the Bottleneck, everything looked fine to him.

'Phew, they're now well-positioned. They have the winning formula! Should I re-join them?'

The Serbian team had been battling for the Holy Grail against all odds. While other teams were regrouping at the Bottleneck base, the Serbian team climbers passed them and Jumic. The day was beautiful, but getting warm. The down suits were too warm and becoming uncomfortable. The sun was sending hot rays from above. Some climbers could barely stand the warmth of the day, dressed as they were.

Serb Milivoj decided to fall out of line for a rest.

"Please take my oxygen bottle for the Serbs. I can't climb anymore," he told the Hap Muhammad, and then stepped aside onto a boulder.

Muhammad, carrying extra oxygen cylinders, looked tired. Milivoj could see his teammates joining the Hap Little Hussein and rallying toward the middle of the Bottleneck using a fixed rope.[114]

Now, Jumic and Wilco were both standing at the bottom of the Bottleneck. Behind them, Cecilia was climbing upward with Rolf. Chris

---

[114] YouTube, Serbia K2 Expedition 2008, Part 5, Disappeared.

overtook Marco, Cas and Gerard. [115] Lars took a snapshot of the last climbers, Marco and Gerard, who were sticking together at the Bottleneck base. [116] Around this time, the last climber, Gerard also took a photograph.[117] Marco knelt down gasping for air. Above him, Chris was climbing toward the bottom part of the Bottleneck.

Chris hopped off the line at the bottom of the Bottleneck and sat beside a boulder. Chhiring joined Chris. They clung together, exchanging quick words as to whether Chris would keep going. Wilco had decided to take off his backpack and cached it with ski poles. He was going to pick it up on his way back. When Wilco resumed climbing, Chris took a photograph of him.[118] Wilco was looking handy.

At the middle of the Bottleneck (around 8150m in altitude), Lars was taking a break while awaiting his teammates below him. While standing on a large boulder, he took another remarkable shot toward the line of climbers below.[119] It showed the downward landscape including the entire Shoulder plus Camp 4 from the middle of the Bottleneck. From this we can figure out who's who.

From above, they were Little Hussein, Dren, Iso, Predrag, Muhammad, Øystein, Hugues, Jehan and Wilco. It is difficult to recognize those further down but probably they were Rolf, Karim, Jumic, Gerard, Cas and Marco. As well, we can see Chris, Chhiring and Milivoj had moved off the line to rest.

---

[115] https://www.flickr.com/photos/25037111@N07/2904775705/in/photostream/

[116] http://abcnews.go.com/Nightline/photos/climbers-fall-death-attempting-k2-11361962/image-11361994

[117] http://eleboo.e-bookshelf.de/products/reading-epub/product-id/3816444/title/Ger%2BMcDonnell%253A%2BHis%2BLife%2B%2526%2BHis%2BDeath%2Bon%2BK2.html?firm=%22THE+COLLINS+PRESS%22

[118] http://mountaineeringsport.blogspot.co.nz/2008/10/k2-disaster.html

[119] http://abcnews.go.com/Nightline/photos/climbers-fall-death-attempting-k2-11361962/image-11362017

Thirty-two

All the climbers were heading toward the middle section of the Bottleneck. The obvious question was, who had done the rope-fixing for the Bottleneck climbing?

Was it Pemba? Unlikely. If we check the relevant images, Pemba, wearing the blue down suit, can be seen climbing below the lead climber. Then, who was the lead climber? Little Pasang? Probably not. The images show the lead climber's suit was close to red in color whereas Little Pasang's was closer to orange. By reviewing matters in this way, an answer was bound to emerge. Was it Alberto? Didn't he wear the red down suit? Right, it was Alberto! That means they had allowed him to take that role, and he had led the climb all the way to the Bottleneck, doing the rope-fixing alone.

The climbing paces were so slow on the Shoulder that Alberto might have become frustrated. He may have thought he was wasting his time, that it would be much better to go ahead as the lead climber. He had patiently awaited his chance near the Bottleneck base. As soon as a bundle of rope became available, he grabbed it and ran into the upper Bottleneck. In the climbers' eyes Alberto was on the sprint. But he couldn't avoid controversy.

He stopped his climb around the middle of the Bottleneck because his rope had run out and he was unable to continue without the help of other climbers. As as soon as they appeared with a further supply of rope, Alberto grabbed it and climbed into the steep gully. Others had to wait. The relevant images and footage[120] show the widened distance between Alberto and the other climbers. The serac was looming over the climbers.

Meanwhile, there was no doubt the Serbian team was wounded. The loss of a valuable Hap at Camp 2 was a big blow. At Camp 3, the team realized they had forgotten to bring the food, and at Camp 4 the lack of a shovel meant no rest. Thus, they started their climb late on D–day. From

---

[120] YouTube, Serbia K2 Expedition 2008, Part 5, Disappeared

the middle of the Bottleneck, the Hap Muhammad had complained about breathing problems caused by altitude sickness.

"No, that's enough! I go down," he declared.

It was another big blow to the team, which was already heavily battered. But, national pride spurred them on. Dren and Predrag each took an oxygen cylinder from the Hap. From that moment, their climbing pace dropped significantly.

In contrast, Wilco, who had deposited his backpack at the bottom of the Bottleneck, felt as light as a bird. Chhiring, carrying a roll of loose rope, had decided to go for the summit. Now, Wilco and Chhiring planned to overtake the other climbers.

The front group of climbers was by then challenging one of the hardest sections on the K2 climb. It was the narrowest gully in the upper Bottleneck. There was a big boulder to overcome before reaching the top of the Bottleneck, while the serac hung threateningly over the climbers' heads. Theoretically, the section should be climbed and traversed quickly. However, the climbers were forced to go slowly, then stop and wait. Alberto was moving slowly over unfamiliar section, requiring the climbers to wait until he completed his climb to the top of the Bottleneck and then fix the rope with an ice-screw. Standstill became routine at that section and most of the climbers took the traffic jam as a chance to remove their backpacks.

When Wilco overtook Jehan and Hugues in the middle section of the Bottleneck, he decided to roll his video camera. Above him was Øystein. Then Wilco turned his camera to Chhiring, who had been continuously chasing him. He filmed until Chhiring passed him. And then, he filmed the group of climbers below him. They were Hugues the oldest, Jehan, Rolf, Marco, Chris, Gerard and Cas. The video would also show Muhammad descending at the base of the Bottleneck.

Cecilia overtook the three Serbs and caught up with Lars in the middle of the Bottleneck. After taking off her red outer suit, she started to chase Little Hussein who was climbing in front of her. As Lars quickly snapped her, a small figure emerged from the top of the big boulder.[122] It was Alberto. His job was done, and it was a proud achievement for him.

"Hey, guys. It's done. Come on!" he shouted.

---

[122] http://gq.globo.com/Cultura/noticia/2013/11/livro-relata-pior-tragedia
-ocorrida-no-k2-segunda-maior-montanha-do-mundo.html

When Pemba started to move up, Alberto took a photograph. The image shows the whole group resuming their climb toward the big boulder at the upper Bottleneck. [123]

From above, they're Pemba, Little Pasang, Little Kim, Hwang, Park, Kim, Go(unseen), Hugues, Iso, Little Hussein, Cecilia, Lars, Dren, Predrag, Øystein, Chhiring (overlapped with Øystein), Wilco, Rolf and Marco. The remainders are difficult to identify but are probably Jehan, Chris, Karim, Gerard and Cas. Jumic was somewhere in there too. He was getting back on track.

---

[123] http://www.barrabes.com/actualidad/noticias/2-5832/tragedia-k2.html

Thirty-three

It was around 10am when Chris went off. When Rolf and Marco had resumed their climb at the bottom of the Bottleneck, Chris had followed them for a while. But on reaching 8150m he saw the looming traffic jam at the big boulder and decided against continuing. He took one shot before his exit.[124]

Pemba was tackling up to climb the big boulder but was wasting his time because he was unable to put his weight on the rope. Alberto had gone to the top of the Bottleneck without fixing any intermediate stations so the rope dragged onto the middle of the boulder. This was yet another problem for the climbers because Alberto's mistake caused a further delay at the upper Bottleneck. The section would soon be jammed.

Rather than waiting until Pemba put an ice-screw on the middle section of the pitch, the Korean team had been seeking a different solution. They decided to climb further to the left side of the boulder by laying another rope (B-rope). Then, they were going to turn to the right to catch Alberto's rope (A-rope). So, another rope crossing over the A-rope was laid and fixed.

The choice divided the climbers. A or B? While the Korean climbers and Hugues took the B-rope, Little Hussein climbed off to the right side with the A-rope, stopping only when he got to the snow obstacle. It took significant time until all the climbers were able to attempt the top boulder, due to the congestion. It was tough climbing. They had to get through this course without making mistakes.

The climbers below had left many relevant images showing these risky struggles. One of the Serbs shot this action with his still camera.[125] The

---

124 http://goalexploration.com/s/K2.html#26

125 http://www.boulderweekly.com/article-9618-k2ufffds-deadliest-day-the-sherpa-perspective.html

snap was included in the video footage titled: Serbia K2 Expedition 2008. Part 5 that was later uploaded on YouTube.[126]

Marco also saw the climbers struggling. Most were hanging on the one anchor and they were too close. Marco took a photograph (*see* p. 120) which shows who was using which rope. Most climbers appeared to be using the B-rope.

From above, it shows Pemba (unseen), Little Pasang (unseen), Hwang, Little Kim, Go, Kim, Hugues, Park and Iso and Chhiring. Little Hussein switched his rope onto B-rope. Next are Cecilia (unseen), Lars and Jumic. They're approaching the boulder. Øystein, Wilco and Predrag are blocked out by Rolf. The remaining group of climbers is out of shot, probably behind Marco. They would be Gerard, Karim and Jehan. But Dren is missing. Was he somewhere in the middle of the traffic jam?

Alberto was still standing on a ledge at the top of the Bottleneck. He'd had more than enough rest there. However, once again, he had to await more rope for the next climb.

The next section was the leftward diagonal passageway before the Traverse. Ahead of that, climbers had to pass a dangerous passageway with a 70° precipice slope. Once through there, the Traverse would start with the crux of cruxes section. Again, Alberto lacked the confidence to challenge this section without rope protection. It would be suicidal to attempt the section alpine style with an ice ax so there was nothing to do but wait for more rope. He knew it would take a long time.

From the bottom to the top, it took almost three hours. When Pemba reached the top of the Bottleneck, he used his ice ax as an anchor. And then Little Pasang finally reached the top. Knowing Pemba wasn't interested in going ahead because of loyalty to his lagging teammates, Alberto handed over his still camera to Little Pasang before resuming his climb.

"Shoot my actions while I climb the crux of cruxes," he demanded.

Maybe this was a good tactic to lure the workforce into trail-breaking on the deeply snowed Traverse and the snowfield? But the bait didn't work. A sudden accident interrupted all plans. Nobody saw the accident coming.

---

[126] Found on May 18, 2014 that the video footage was removed. Why? This was curious.

Thirty-four

Alberto was successful in crossing the diagonal passageway. He was now climbing toward the 70° exposed slope (*see* p. 119). It was at the beginning of the Traverse. While Little Pasang was waiting for his teammates, he took shots of Alberto fixing the ice-screw on the upper section of the exposed slope.[127]

Back at upper Bottleneck, the passage was narrower. Through it, the climbers were reaching the top of the Bottleneck. An exposed place, there was no place for climbers to hide so it gradually became crowded.

"Move! Quick! I need more solid footing." This was a common call.

The place became critically and dangerously backlogged. No one could pass. If there was one slip, a climber might fall away. Jumic then joined Korean team climbers at the top. How could he be there? How was it possible? Did he take a shortcut?

Meanwhile, the front team was at the diagonal narrow passageway, which was one of the most slippery sections. Hwang was in charge. The squeezed climbers started to climb across the passageway one by one. When Go and Kim were about to take their turn, the Norwegian climber Øystein jumped in front of them. He had been an underdog from day one. It was his third K2 expedition. He was the last climber in the team while climbing the upper Bottleneck and was determined to make it to the front of the group. How? By direct climbing? By bypassing the top of the Bottleneck? Some climbers might have been impressed by his unexpected interception but most were annoyed because they were forced to stay longer on the uncomfortable edge.

The climb became more dangerous. Pemba decided to halt until Wilco joined him. He needed to talk. When Little Pasang was crossing the passageway, others were about to jump in behind him and engage in freestyle climbing. His teammates were already climbing the exposed slope to reach the main section of the Traverse.

---

[127] http://www.barrabes.com/actualidad/noticias/2-5832/tragedia-k2.html

It was 11.15am.

"AaaaaRrrrr!"

The sudden screams made climbers' hearts sink. Everyone was stunned and frightened, their adrenalin pumping. Everyone could sense something bad had happened. Some thought they glimpsed a climber tumbling down into the void. Little Pasang looked back.

"Accident?"

"Someone fell down!"

Some saw the fallen climber tumbling down once more, only to stop at the bottom of the Bottleneck.

"He fell, again!"

"Is he alive?"

It was the Serb climber Dren Mandic. Dren was the first to die in the 2008 K2 season. Later, there were many theories, explanations, testimonies and words written about the accident. There were also some compelling stories about it. But it transpired there were many holes in the explanations about Dren's fall.[128] No one raised serious questions. Why was that?

What triggered the downfall? How had the fall happened from the Bottleneck? Did Dren try to do something out of the ordinary? Since it was the toughest climb for everyone, it would have been proper to check the moment of Dren's fall by comparing his positions *before* and *after* the fall.

Before falling (climbers were on the top of the Bottleneck).

From above: Go, Kim, Hugues, Chhiring, Iso, Park, Little Hussein, Cecilia, Lars, Jumic, Øystein, Wilco, Predrag, Rolf and Marco. Dren does not seem to be in the photograph. Had the extra load slowed him down, forcing him to join the last group of Jehan, Gerard, Cas and Karim?

After falling.

From above: (on the Traverse side) Aberto, Jumic, Little Kim, Hwang, Øystein, Park, Go, Kim, and Little Pasang. And Cecilia with backpack has been left alone on the dangerous passageway after Dren's fall. The rest of climbers were on the top of the Bottleneck or hanging below on the big boulder before reaching the top.

Before his fall, Dren was on the dangerous passageway with Cecilia. Before that, he was one of the climbers hanging below or around the big boulder (*see* p. 120). How could he suddenly turn up ahead of Cecilia in the

---

[128] http://www.everestnews.com/pak2008/k22008sadnews081220080101.htm

passageway? Could he have overtaken the other climbers by freestyle climbing?

While hanging around or below the top boulder, Dren might have felt uncomfortable on the rope because all the climbers were dependent on the single thin line. And he might have felt crushed by the extra load. Remember, he was carrying the extra cylinder. Maybe his desire to offload the weight as soon as possible caused him to take a shortcut?

When he reached the rope on the passageway, he would have realized that not only was the surface slippery but also his load was virtually killing him. At that point he would probably have changed his mind in favour of descending to the opposite site—the top of the Bottleneck. Cecilia was following him. At an altitude of 8200m, seeing her on that dangerous passageway must have been alarming for him. Since he would not have dared to return upward, he had to face the problem and so would have unclipped his rope clamp.

'Pass with care!'

While he was watching or passing, he suddenly lost his footing. He tried to grab the rope, to grab anything, but failed. He went down.

Sunrise on 2008 K2 Summit, as seen from Broad Peak

(*Credit Andy Selters*)

After the final meeting on July 25

Standing in the front row: Kim Jae-Su (L), (Kneeling in the front row) Hwang Dong-Jin, Go Mi-Young, Karim Meherban, Shaheen Baig (in some pictures, cook Nadir Ali Shar), Wilco Van Rooijen (L), Little Hussein, Jehan Baig, the Serbian team's assistant cook Nisar.
Middle from the left: Robert Goh (L), Dren Mandic, Eric Meyer, Chhiring Dorje, Chris Warner, Mike Farris (L), Milivoj Erdeljan, Miodrag Jovovic (L), the Serbian team's liaison officer Captain Sabir Ali, Muhammad Khan.
Back row: Shon Byung-Woo, Hugues d'Aubarede, Pemba Gyalje, Marco Confortola (L), Roberto Manni, Predrag Zagorac, Iso Planic, Rolf Bae, Lars Flato Nessa.

(To see this Internet image above, *Google Search* using the keyword "2008 K2 Disaster.")[129]

---

[129] http://abcnews.go.com/Nightline/photos/climbers-fall-death-attempting-k2-11361962/image-11362174

The plans and climbing routes

Left: Cesen route / **Right**: Abruzzi route

(*Illustrated by J.I.Jeon*)

The Bottleneck and beyond, from Camp 4 at 7800 meters on the
Shoulder of the Abruzzi ridge
(*Credit Lars Nessa Flato*)

August 1, 2008 (Summit day)

They're climbing the boulder to reach the top of the Bottleneck.

From above, this illustration shows Pemba (unseen), Little Pasang (unseen), Hwang (1), Little Kim (2), Go (3), Kim (4), Hugues (5), Park (6), Iso (7) and Chhiring (8). Little Hussein (9) switched his rope onto the B–rope. Next are Cecilia (unseen), Lars (10) and Jumic (11). Øystein, Wilco and Predrag are blocked out by Rolf (12). The remaining group of climbers is out of shot, probably behind Marco. They would be Gerard, Karim and Jehan.

But Dren is missing. Was he somewhere in the middle of the traffic jam?

(*Illustration based on the photograph of Marco Confortola*)[130]

---

[130] http://www.turismo.it/multimedia/art/giorni-di-ghiaccio-sul-k2-id-5948/ p. 64-65, *Marco Confortola Giorni Di Ghiaccio*

Pakistani Hap Jehan Baig fell and slid down the east side of the ice slope. This fatal accident occurred around 2.40pm on August 1. There were in total twenty climbers on the last part of the Traverse and beyond. The summit's still a long way from there. It'll take them three to five hours more. And, then, descending... in darkness?

On that day, eighteen climbers summited the top of K2, but nine more climbers perished on the descent.

(*Illustration based on the photograph of 2008 Flying Jump Korea K2 Expedition*)

10am on August 2 (Rescue day)

This photograph remains one of the controversal photographs interpreting the whole events of the day.

(*Credit International Norit K2 Expedition*)

Thirty-five

"Who killed Dren?"

The accident had cast a shadow across the rest of the climbers in general. What was the aftermath? Everybody looked at everybody else. Most of the climbers on the top of the Bottleneck were just standing on their footings and looking down in the direction where Dren had fallen.

"That poor guy... This is tragic..."

"Deja vu!" someone remarked sadly.

Last year, Nima the Nepalese Sherpa had fallen down here and died. But most of the climbers had kept on toward the top.

Dren's fall had triggered doubts about the climb. Doom had set in but either no one saw it as a deadly sign, or they chose to ignore it.

Kim was on the bottom section of the steep, icy Traverse slope when he sensed something was wrong below. He soon learned of the accident. But now a dice for the women's fourteen 8000er race was spinning. Kim was determined. So he shouted to the line "Keep going!", and also to Little Pasang who was on the bottom part of the exposed slope.

"Little Pasang, just hurry up!"

When Little Pasang started his climb by following his teammates. He took a shot of the team's activity with his still camera.[131] Jumic was in the lead and he was climbing onto the main route of the Traverse, carrying some white rope on his backpack. Hwang, Little Kim who had unzipped his upper suit, Øystein who wore just a lightweight blue top, Go, Park and Kim were following him.

Then, Lars was at the top of the Bottleneck. He also took two continuous shots of Øystein on the 70° precipice slope. Øystein was in full trottle using an ice ax and ski stick, and he was about to overtake Park,

---

[131] http://foreigntravel.tistory.com/m/post/1424

who was struggling to pick his ice axe up by his legs. It was tethered by the rope with his harness.[132]

Alberto was far above the slope. But again, he ran out of rope. Again, he had to wait for the climbers. And, of course, his camera, too. Sitting on the deep snow slope, he could see the climbers and urged them on.

"Come on, lads!!!"

At this stage he didn't know of the accident.

Later, one of the Camp 4 climbers learned of it. Roberto sensed something strange in the movement of the Bottleneck climbers. He had been watching their progress. When he realized, he screamed his message.

"Someone fell from the Bottleneck!"

The Camp 4 climbers who had been resting in their tents rushed out in shock. Nick came out first. Crouching, he started to take photographs of the event with his still camera.[133] The first thing Fred did was to grip the camcorder and turn it on. He came out wondering what had gone on.

"What's happening?"

"What do you see?"

Someone responded to him saying, "Calm down. Calm down..."

Fred rolled his video camera wildly trying to find the fallen climber. But he could not capture him.

"Where is he?"

" . . . . . "

Fred wanted to record the momentous footage, but he couldn't focus on the fallen climber. Instead, he passed his camcorder down to Nick. Fred's focus returned to the Bottleneck, trying to find the object. Instead, he could see the group of climbers. Cecilia was in the middle of the dangerous passageway.[134] She was struggling to go upward from there.

---

[132] http://www.aftenbladet.no/nyheter/lokalt/Isras-grunnen-til-K2-ulykken-2010559.html

[133] http://www.outsideonline.com/adventure-travel/asia/pakistan/A-Few-False-Moves.html

K2 - A Cry From The Top Of The World [DVD] [2009]

[134] http://www.businessinsider.com.au/the-summit-2008-k2-tragedy-2013-10#according-to-van-rooijen-there-was-a-group-meeting-among-expedition-leaders-the-night-before-the-climb-to-decide-how-they-were-going-to-tackle-the-last-part-of-the-mountain-as-one-team-12

Meanwhile, there was a climber down from the near Bottleneck base. Dren had fallen nearby. Who was this climber? Surely, he was one of those who turned back. Did he hear the screams and see Dren's fall?

Fred's camcorder also caught him briefly. He was now near the upper Shoulder, which meant he was coming down toward Camp 4 regardless of the accident, and all the while climbers from above and below were wildly shooting pictures in the vicinity of the fallen climber. Who was he?

Possibly the tragedy should have caused another major delay. Yet it didn't deter the climbers. Clearly, "summit fever" had formed and prevailed.

Hwang halted his team. Jumic and Little Kim were at the mouth of the Traverse then. They also realized that Alberto's rope finished there.

"The section ahead is stiff and looks dangerous to climb without rope-protection. Let's install rope," said Hwang.

Øystein also had some ropes.

At this point, the identity of the climber who crossed the passageway after Cecilia remained unknown.

And for the front group, the rope-fixing proved another setback and caused a further hour's delay in their expedition. While awaiting the rope-fixing, Øystein took a photograph. This one provided not only the answer to the question: 'Who was the climber after Cecilia?' but also some clues to the expedition following Dren's fall. Someone cropped the image smartly! However, Hugues had crossed the passageway. Was he the climber after Cecilia? In any event he'd pushed on since the rope was there. According to the photograph the climbers ahead of him were Cecilia, Little Pasang, Go and Kim.[135]

There was one more climber who crossed the passageway. Surprisingly, it was the Serb, Iso! Apparently, he might have witnessd something. So he must have run to get Cecilia after Dren's fall. And now, the two were almost whispering[136] about the matter seriously while the other squeezed climbers were simply climbing onward up the Traverse slope!

Though there are many stories about the accident, this fact has never been made public. This is curious.

Then, four climbers docked on the top of the Bottleneck. They were Lars, Pemba, Jehan and the Serb Predrag. Lars was at the far right end of the top.

---

[135] http://moveablefest.com/moveable_fest/2013/10/nick-ryan-summit.html

[136] p. 124 *The Summit* by Pat Falvey / Pemba Gyalje Sherpa

He was sitting comfortably drinking water and watching the whispered conference between Cecilia and Iso at the crux among cruxes in K2. Overhead was the big threat—the overhanging serac. Lars might have wondered whether the expedition was over at this point.

Meanwhile, Pemba was fishing. Reeling and winding back a rope line, it was a form of rock-fishing on the top of the K2 Bottleneck.[137] At 8150m on the Bottleneck, why? Where had the rope line come from? Nothing seemed impossible after the accident. With great effort, Pemba almost hauled Wilco to the top.

Hugues' Hap Jehan was preparing to go down. His job was done when he'd handed over the spare oxygen bottles to Hugues.

Predrag, the Serb climber was about to abseil down. Before going down to the scene where Dren fell, he wanted to check in with Iso, who was still conferring with Cecilia.

Suddenly, Cecilia started to move upwards. That meant that Lars had to quickly catch up to her as his team leader. When Lars and then Wilco were crossing the passageway, their Norwegian teammate Øystein took another photograph toward Lars.

Five climbers were clinging to the rocks and ice at the top of the Bottleneck. Gerard had unzipped his top suit and tied it around his waist. At his right side, Little Hussein was eyeing the Traverse. Next was Pemba. Chhiring and Marco were watching from the right end.[138]

Pemba then finished his fishing. Had he released the rope, letting it fall? Or put it back in his backpack? Cas was taking his final step onto the top of the Bottleneck to join the group. The climber below him was probably Rolf.

Marco was hurrying to approach the passageway for his crossing. He had to pass all the climbers who were on the top of the Bottleneck. When he got there, Rolf was already in front of him. And then Gerard was on the way to cross the passageway after Marco.[139]

When the last three climbers—Little Hussein, Cas and Chhiring—were crossing the passageway at the same time, the thin rope looked dangerous. Wilco videoed the scene.[140]

---

[137] p. 124 *The Summit* by Pat Falvey / Pemba Gyalje Sherpa

[138] http://www.readersdigest.co.nz/Book_news_September_2011

[139] http://abcnews.go.com/Nightline/photos/climbers-fall-death-attempting-k2-11361962/image-11362189

[140] http://smartfilm.blogspot.co.nz/2013/10/out-in-theaters-summit.html

All had apparently crossed the passageway. Was the top of the Bottleneck emptied? No, a climber was still there. It was Pemba.[141]

'Everyone has gone upward! I'm alone. What should I do? Go up or go down? That's the question.'

Back at the front group,[142] Alberto had disappeared around the corner. Jumic kept laying and fixing the rope-works. Kim and Go were changing their oxygen cylinders. Probably, Hugues and Karim also changed their oxygen cylinders.

Finally, Chris K returned to Camp 4 and joined his teammates Eric and Fred. Chris carried a radio so Eric could make a call to Chhiring, but without success.

While still looking the place where Dren had fallen, Roberto came to them and pointed to it with his finger. As soon as Eric got there, he relayed it to Chris, tapping his shoulder.

"Yeah, right there at the edge."

Fred's camera was rolling to get it. Dren had fallen to 8020m. Eric wanted to make radio contact with Chhiring. But there was no reply. The day was warm so Chris stripped off his down suit and tied it around his waist. He was wearing a black jacket with black gloves and was still sweating. While Chris was resting beside Eric, a radio call came in from Chhiring. His voice was quick and excited.

"Yeah, Chhiring, this is Eric, Camp 4, over," Eric responded. "Chhiring, eh, I understand that you and Pemba are climbing. Are you in the lead, and has there been an accident? Over."

"Dren was moving," Chhiring answered back.

"Is he in the rock?" Chris asked.

Then, Roberto came again and pointed out the place for him.

"Yes, there he is! There's the rock."

"Yeah," Chris answered.

"Down," Roberto said again.

"Yeah," Eric responded.

"Down," Roberto said again.

"Yeah. Chhiring says he's moving," Eric said.

"Is everybody coming down?" Chris put the question at some point.

141 http://www.watchorpass.com/2013/10/release-date-october-4-2013-very.html

142 http://www.outsideonline.com/adventure-travel/asia/pakistan/A-Few-False-Moves.html

"Ask," he directed Eric softly.

"Chhiring, do you know if... if everyone is coming down at this point? Over," Eric radioed back.[143]

However, such a question was too late. They were heading toward the middle section of the Traverse. And there was not a big conversation about the accident or about turning around.

---

[143] http://www.businessinsider.com.au/the-summit-2008-k2-tragedy-2013-10#some-climbers-at-camp-4-saw-the-fall-and-sent-a-rescue-team-to-recover-mandic-whom-they-thought-was-still-alive-22

Thirty-six

Kim and Go were back to catch up with their team as soon as they changed oxygen cylinders. Their batteries were recharged. Naturally, the other climbers' pace had slowed down. And now Cecilia had to pass Little Pasang, who was hanging the empty cylinders on an ice-screw. While Wilco was approaching Little Pasang, Lars, Rolf, Marco, Gerard, Cas and Chhiring were crawling up the steep exposed slope.[144]

Dren had fallen from the top of Bottleneck (8200m) to the bottom, at 8020m, a fall of 180m. When his teammate Predrag reached Dren, he was lifeless with blood on his head. Camp 4 climbers didn't recognize what had happened and were still confused.

"Is Dren still alive?"

"Maybe."

"Wow, this is history and there's a doctor in Camp 4. Shall we go up?"

Most of the Camp 4 climbers didn't like this idea. When Eric entered his tent, Fred followed him, filming. Meanwhile, where were the Serb turnaround climber Milivoj and the Hap Muhammad? Had they gone down toward Camp 3, already? Didn't they know about their teammates' shakiness?

Most of the climbers were on the open Traverse route under the serac. The climbing pace was slow, sometimes at a stand-still and sometimes moving. Lars was waiting. He snapped Rolf posing with a smile while climbing. Rolf looked tired, and the supplementary oxygen was running from behind his back into his nose through a tiny tube. Wilco didn't like to waste time in such a scary place. While waiting, he called Maarten of NLBC to report the news of Dren's fall. Within a few minutes, Maarten updated the news on the Norit blog.

---

[144] https://www.flickr.com/photos/25037111@N07/2904775669/in/photostream/

"Much to my regret I have to inform you that early this morning an accident occurred in the Bottleneck. The messages are erratic and chaotic but as far as I know now a (supposing) Serbian climber fell several hundred meters down the Bottleneck."

The Traverse was the coolest place. But most of the climbers had no time to enjoy its beauty. It was suppressed by the depressing thought: "I am beneath the dangerous serac!" And they were surrounded by the abyss, with slippery snow.

Hanging on a rope, Wilco quickly turned on his video camera and filmed the icy high serac walls above him, and filmed the climbers in action ahead of him. Then, he boldly turned his camera back on Rolf and Lars. Rolf was holding together Lars' ice-ax. Wilco conducted a sudden interview on the Traverse.

"How are you?" Wilco asked.

"Good. But not a great day today! A hard day for me today!" Rolf declared.

"Yes. It's not a good day," Wilco repeated. Was it because of the accident?

Behind Rolf, Norit teammate Gerard was standing still and Cas was sitting. Chhiring was at the end of the line. He was now resting on the ice-screw where the empty cylinders were hanging. If something happened to the thin rope from which everyone was hanging, he would be safe. Clever! The serac over the Bottleneck and the various small mountains of China provided the backdrop.

The Korean Team 2 was climbing toward Camp 4, approaching the top of the slope below the camp. Even though they couldn't see the summit team's progress, they were keen to hear about it. They knew about the accident from the chaotic radio communications and had probably met several turnaround climbers. They kept checking the summit climbers' tweets by radio. Singaporean team members who started with the Korean team had considered quitting their climb because of inadequate acclimatization. They would soon go back to Camp 3.

Lone climber Alberto was not part of the climbers anymore. He waited for the climbers a long time but must have realized the rope fixing and changing oxygen cylinders would cause too much delay in his climb. So he had decided to go on the Traverse without any rope. Now, he was climbing on the last serac section of the Traverse.

"This is tough!"

This section was one of the hardest parts; difficult to climb with an ice ax. He soon became exhausted. But he was a lucky man. He met with an old rope fixed at 8320m. It was 8mm rope connected with a piton. Probably a year old at least. Outwardly, it looked all right, but it wasn't trustworthy, having endured the wind and the strong UV rays at that high altitude. So, hacking hard at the slope with his ice ax and making sure of his three points, Alberto had to be careful in using the rope. At the top of the slope, he would reach to the deep snowfield by turning to the right (*see* p. 119).

Back at Camp 4, Fred and Eric had decided to go up to Dren. The noonday sun was just overhead. So, did they think that everything would be all right for them? While Eric was packing his backpack with emergency stuff and medicine, Fred and Chris could watch the line of twenty climbers on the Traverse, dwarfed by the serac. Fred shot the scene with his video camera. And Chris took photos.[145]

Back at the Traverse, lead climber Jumic was heading onto the upper section. In half an hour, the rest of climbers would follow his footsteps. Jumic had to wait for more rope for another pitch. However, the supporting climbers—Little Kim, Hwang, Park—had stopped climbing. Why? Were they changing their oxygen cylinders? The exact reason was unknown. Øystein took another rest behind them. He could be a momentum-switcher by overtaking them. But he couldn't because: first, no one could support him from the back so he could go after his own style, like Alberto. And, second, he had a team behind to work together.

Instead, he had his half-time for lunch while waiting for his teammates. The next climber below Øystein was Go. She was leaning forward. Kim behind was standing, probably urging her to keep climbing up. Behind them was Hugues. Cecilia was the next one to be leaning forward. And behind her was Karim who was marching upward. Little Pasang and Wilco were in a rush. After filming, Wilco might realize that time was passing quickly. As noon had been and gone, just waiting was not a good tactic.

"I can't wait anymore. I have to top K2, today!" he said.

Behind Wilco, the last group of climbers—Lars, Rolf, Marco, Gerard, Cas, and Chhiring—were following him. There was a lone climber below the last group: Pemba. He was coming up from the bottom section of the Traverse. Dren's fall was not a good sign for the Himalaya veteran and he

---

[145] http://abcnews.go.com/Nightline/photos/climbers-fall-death-attempting-k2-11361962/image-11362226

was not sure of today's climb, considering delaying the climbing time. Squashing his hesitation might hurt him but he finally decided to continue climbing, reluctantly.

'I'll have a look,' he may have thought. 'I still have enough daylight to turn around.'

By contrast, a Serbian team's Hap, Little Hussein, turned back! He was climbing down just below the heart-shaped boulder. [146] He had also hesitated a long time after crossing the passageway, despite Dren's fall, and was the only climber who knew the entire route for the summit pyramid. He was also the last one to uphold the team's pride, but had to turn and go down since his team's leader had declared:

"Our expedition is over!"

---

[146] http://abcnews.go.com/Nightline/photos/climbers-fall-death-attempting-k2-11361962/image-11362226

Thirty-seven

Wilco had chased the front group by overtaking other climbers vigorosly, while Kim considered changing his team's tactics.

'The hardest section is ahead... It's the time to change the lead climber,' he thought. 'Jumic must be exausted.'

When he rechecked Little Pasang he looked all right.

"Little Pasang! Go and lead!" he shouted.

When Little Pasang came upward, he had to overtake several climbers using X–nudges at times. Kim also had to mobilize his team harder.

"Come on guys!"

Back at Camp 4, Fred was heading toward the Serbian team at the bottom of the Bottleneck. Eric would soon follow him. Chris, Roberto and Nick had decided to go down to the lower camps. It was almost 12.40pm. When Eric started his climb, Chris took a photograph. It also captured the climbers on the Traverse.[147]

On the Traverse, the climbers divided into three groups. The first group had five climbers who were heading up the steeper slope with deep snow, making for the last serac. The second group was on the middle of the Traverse, following the first group. They stretched out like a long train. The last group was Chhiring and Pemba who were now climbing together. Chhiring must have slowed down to wait for Pemba.

Wilco was at full throttle. He was fighting for the top by leapfrogging anyone whenever there were gaps. Cas saw him and decided to make a film.[148]

Now, Chhiring was in front of Cas. He must have overtaken him while Cas was trying to set his camera into video mode on the foot-deep snow slope.

---

[147] http://goalexploration.com/s/K2.html#27

[148] https://www.youtube.com/watch?v=oF87ZZ0kKx4

Karim had fallen away from Hugues. He was now climbing behind Gerard, but before Chhiring. He looked to be having some problem with his oxygen apparatus. While still moving upward, he was maneuvering it. Above him was Marco. And above Marco were Rolf and Lars. In front of them was Cecilia. Øystein was now behind his teammates and Marco. His backpack looked empty. He might have transferred the spare oxygen cylinders to his teammate. Above Cecilia were Hugues, Kim and Go. Wilco was climbing there, in front of Go.[149] Wilco looked like he was leading, but in fact there were five more climbers in front of him—Jumic, Little Kim, Park, Hwang and Little Pasang. Jumic was still in charge.

Where was Alberto? He was at a different altitude. After climbing the deep snowfield, he took time to cool down under the lee of a small serac at 8450m. Above him was the summit track, known as the sickle-shaped route, and then the summit ridge, which was the last short ridge under the summit.

---

[149] https://www.youtube.com/watch?v=oF87ZZ0kKx4

Thirty-eight

The Korean Team 2 climbers had made it over the last overhang slope at 12.40pm. They could see a front part of the summit team's climbers. A lone climber was resting under the lee of a small serac at 8450m. They also could see several climbers who were the first group moving toward the upper section of the Traverse.

"Oh, my goodness! Are they still climbing along the Traverse? Let's take some photographs to find out Who's Who!" said No. 2 Kim.

The first five climbers were in the frame. When they zoomed in on the images, Shon said:

"Isn't that Jumic leading? And then, Little Kim, Park, Hwang and Little Pasang? Is the next one Wilco?"[150]

Wilco had kept pushing on, but his abilty to overtake was not limitless. He was worn out, and the upper section of the Traverse was the most dangerous section for passing.

Back at the Bottleneck base, the Serb Iso had almost made it to the scene of Dren's fall. His teammates were in a panic.

"What can we do with the body?" said Iso.

Nobody knows who decided, but they quickly hatched a plan to lower the body to Camp 4.

Around the same time, Little Hussein met Jehan, the Hugues' Hap. He was sitting a few meters above the bottom of the Bottleneck. They would join the team at the Bottleneck base where Serb climbers were moaning.

Little Hussein was also lost his words. But . . .

"Bring the body down from here?" questioned Little Hussein.

At last, Fred arrived at the Bottleneck base. It had taken him one-and-half hours. Was it about 1.40pm? Predrag and Iso were devastated. The Serbs must have inwardly wept bitterly over the loss of Dren. Little Hussein and Jehan were just sitting behind his body, which they had half-

---

[150] http://blog.daum.net/flyingjump/58

covered with a red plastic sheet. They had tried to recover the body a little further down from the original scene. Fred also learned they wanted to continue with the body recovery mission to Camp 4. It was understandable, but they were pushing their luck by taking unnecessary risks. While the climbers sat or stood around Dren's body, staring blankly, Fred took out his camera, turned it on in video mode and started filming the scene. It irritated one of the Serbs who was in deep distress.

"What are you doing?" said Iso.

Fred had his reasons. Predrag listened and then testified to Dren's fall, death and his reaction.

"He hit the rock, lost control, keep falling for 200 more meters, and stopped. And then I started coming down. There were maybe two guys below me, so I came down pretty fast, maybe 10 minutes. He was wrapped in rope and just giving no signs of life. Already very pale and gray, cuts on the head, black nose, broken, blood from mouth . . . "

"Finished," Fred said.

"Totally finished, almost," Predrag repeated.

They intended waiting for Eric who was coming slowly. It must have been so steep for him. All were shaking with cold and hunger. Fred offered them chocolate bars.

Back at the Traverse, Little Pasang finally managed to take the lead. He was in charge of the rope-fixing for the dangerous section. He climbed toward the end slope, which curved up to the right and led to the deep lower snowfield. He was following Alberto's footsteps but soon realized his rope would run out. Then, Little Pasang saw an old rope fixed at 8320m. He tried to tie his rope to the old rope.

The climbers below him had almost escaped the scare of the serac. But another bumper-to-bumper situation was going to happen at the last serac section, which had 70m vertical slope.

"Oh, no! Another traffic jam at this slope!" said someone.

Just waiting and doing nothing had become one of the routine but terrible things about that day's climb. They had no choice but to hang about until Little Pasang had fixed the rope. It was another ordeal at a dangerous and dizzy slope.

As he gradually tied knots with the rope, the line of climbers could move higher. Their climbing was in slow motion but most still wanted to beat the odds for success. Everyone was complaining inwardly about the other climbers' skills. 'Hey, guys! Hurry up. You're so slow,' they wanted to yell out.

At last, Rolf declared he would not try to top K2. He was worn out and had almost consumed his oxygen supply.

Oxygen shortage had been predicted since the delay in climbing. The oxygen had flowed through each climber's body but, what would happen if it suddenly ran out? First, the psychological impact would be huge. And second, they would climb in a hypoxic state. If they experienced any high-altitude sickness, nobody knew what would happen. Rolf might need to go down immediately, but he insisted on waiting until Cecilia went down from the top.

Then, Alberto woke up from his power nap. He was delighted to see two climbers on the snowfield. Although it was getting late, he desperately needed his camera to take summit pictures for his sponsors. But Alberto saw how slowly the climbers were moving. Surely, they must be exhausted and would need to take a break. Then, he realized he had not time for a camera since he was tentless at Camp 4. He would have to go down to Camp 3 after topping out.

Thirty-nine

It was around 1.40pm when Big Pasang and Tsering of the Korean Team 2 arrived to Camp 4, and around 2.20pm by the time all the Korean Team 2 climbers finally arrived back at camp. As soon as they dropped their backpacks, they started to search for their teammates who were heading to the summit. One of the Koreans was snapping pictures.

The summit party climbers were at the last serac slope of the Traverse. Indeed, it was a murderous traffic jam, highly risky! [151] Some were heading to the snowfield despite such a late climb. It was an awful moment for Team 2 climbers, as well. Their summit chance might be blown already.

They could check the images to know who was who in the summit teams. Alberto had just started his climb toward the sickle-shaped summit track. That was one.

Two climbers were in the diagonal ascent on the snowfield. They were probably Little Pasang and Hwang. That made three.

Next was Jumic. He stopped to help other climbers onto the top of the slope. All the climbers under him were dependent on a single rope. After Park, Jumic was drawing Little Kim to the upper slope. Wilco, Kim and Go were waiting their turn. That made nine.

There were in total twenty climbers on the Traverse beyond. So the remaining climbers should equal eleven. They must have been (from above) Cecilia, Lars, Chhiring, Pemba, Marco, Hugues, Øystein, Karim, Gerard, Cas and Rolf. Hugues was waiting for Karim, who was off the line fixing his oxygen apparatus.

It was around 2.30pm when Australian Paul of the American International team arrived at Camp 4. Eric was a few minutes away from joining the group, having left Fred with the Serb team climbers.

---

[151] http://foreigntravel.tistory.com/m/post/1424

Regarding the body recovery mission, the four climbers Predrag and Iso, Fred and Jehan decided to lower Dren's body. Little Hussein was going to follow them carrying backpacks.

But they stopped their mission after just a few meters. It was no easy job. Each person had to be careful not to lose their balance and to go in one direction. If a climber went off, the whole group would be in danger, probably sliding down onto the China side.

Eric had almost reached the Bottleneck base. He was just a few feet under the group and trying to steer his climb onto the left side to avoid the route down being taken by the group.

And then, suddenly, the Hap Jehan Baig fell. Fred felt Jehan almost crash onto him. Did Jehan lost his footing by a sudden dragging force or was he having trouble breathing, since he had suffered altitude sickness since that morning?

Watching the story on a TV program *Treacherous Mountain Climbing*[152] on ABC Nightline, a blogger 'bigrigjim' sharply pointed out:

"Just a minute, the guy shouted "release the rope" over and over and the dude says "he just lost his grip on the rope". Talk about denial!!!"

Jehan was slipping and sliding down the east side of the ice slope (*see* p. 121). Everyone was stunned, and shouted to him at the top of their voices:

"Stop! Stop!"

They shouted his name, crying, but it was no use. He didn't stop. Even he didn't try to arrest his fall. He slid away and disappeared into the China side abyss. Everyone was shattered, just standing there in shock, silent, seeing the void that had swallowed Jehan.

This fatal accident occurred around 2.40pm, and Jehan was the second victim in the 2008 K2 season. One of the Korean Team 2 climbers at Camp 4 captured the fatal moment with his camera.[153] Fred was around 15m apart from the group but watching on, just above Jehan.

With the accident, Fred and Eric, in shock, decided to go back to Camp 4. Serbian team climbers wrapped Dren's body in the Serbian flag and secured it with an ice ax. It was 7900m to the right side of the slope from Camp 4.

---

[152] http://abcnews.go.com/Nightline/video/treacherous-mountain-climbing-11371713

[153] p. 121 in this book

Forty

Where was Alberto climbing at the 2.40pm? He was still heading toward the summit track over the snowfield. The climbers on the deep snowfield could see him.

2.40pm was also a critical time for the other climbers, since it could be the turnaround time. From there to the summit was 250m. The first part of the snowfield was open slope, heavily laden. No more fixed rope was necessary and there were no more human obstacles from there on. Anyone who was the strongest could go first, but in alpine style.

Before going for it, the climbers were going to take breaks, since climbing the top rope section had worn them out. They also needed to wait for their colleagues to further reassess the situation and regroup.

Thus, it would take more three or four hours to reach the top of K2.[154] Some climbers were still coming up from the last serac slope. It meant they had to get back to Camp 4 to avoid a dangerous climb down in total darkness. Big decisions were required.

The group's mentality was still fixated on reaching the top. Oblivious to time and hunger, most of the climbers might have thought:

'Today's weather is too good.'

'We might not have another opportunity.'

'This is it!'

Some might have thought: 'Now we're so close, I don't want to miss out on the Holy Grail.'

Time was flying. It was already 3pm. Little Pasang's work was probably done. He was heading toward the summit track.

At this point, Øystein had to swallow his ego. He decided to turn back and had no headlamp for his descent in the darkness.

Wilco was worn out. He needed more break than he'd expected. Not only had he burned himself out by overtaking climbers in the Traverse but

---

[154] *see* p. 116 in this book.

he had also dropped his water flask into the void. It was a mistake that cost him dear. While Wilco was waiting for his teammates to regroup, the Korean team climbers resumed their climb toward the summit track.

Since Jumic had to go up to catch up with his team, the last group of climbers was left behind on the precipice slope. These kinds of mixed feelings and frustration might have brought up the question about turning around.

'Should I continue this climb?'

It was a serious matter, choosing life or death. If they chose to go up at this late time of the day, first, no one had bivvy gear; second, though there were guide rails they knew the lifelines were not strong enough. Dangerous! So, they might have thought about turning back.

"But, until we climbed here... It would be okay if we get over these last hurdles," said someone.

The climbers had a huge problem. Someone should at least have shouted:

"We have to TURNAROUND!"

But, Marco was shouting from below:

"The first climbers in K2 have arrived at the summit at 6pm!"

All of this could have added to the pressure, since this could be the last chance that season.

'Yeah, I know it. I'll be okay since many are climbing together.'

This kind of pack mentality has driven many climbers' luck, even though they must have known the odds of surviving would be grim in the reality of a frozen darkness.

Little Kim's speed had visibly slowed. He was also burned out and probably his oxygen had run out too.

Here, the climbers who could face the same problem were all oxygen users, that is, all the Korean team climbers, two Norwegian climbers, Chhiring, Hugues and Karim. But the Norwegian team had a different oxygen system. They could adjust the oxygen supply more precisely by controlling the valve. Chhiring had never used oxygen; he just carried it in case.

Since all were exhausted, the climbers using oxygen could move faster.

The Norwegians were a team of two. Their small size meant they could make quick moves. Lars just came to K2 to see how high he could get, but now he was one of the front climbers. He had overtaken most of the Korean team members. Cecilia was chasing him.

Forty-one

"The last 150m!"

It was Alberto's glorious approach. He had fought with gravity while climbing the crown. Unbelievable.

Finally, carving slightly into the right, and then suddenly turning into the left, he could reach the summit ridge. He had already exhausted his physical strength but his mental fortitude was strong. Slow but steady.

He forgot time. He was in eternity. When he finally reached the wide area where many mountains and the northern skies spread out, he burst out:

"I summit K2!!!"

It was around 4pm, when the forty-eight-year-old Spaniard Aberto Zerain summited the top of K2. He was the first K2 summiteer of the season. It had taken more than 14 hours from Camp 4.

The view from the top was spectacular. It delivered breathtaking scenery. The high and low peaks were all under K2. It was a more pleasant experience to have a 360 degree view. Alberto could see a short distance beyond the summit, to the north ridge and China over east. Tibet was in the far distance. To the south-east were the three towering 8000-class mighty mountains: Broad Peak the 12th highest mountain in the world, Gasherbrum I the 11th, Gasherbrum II the 13th, and many 7000m and 6000m mountaintops brought low. To the west, the Karakorum Range and Hindukush ranges over the Mustaf peak stretched out in a rectangular shape. The combination of glaciers and snow peaks was wonderful.

It was unlucky he couldn't take a photograph of this majestic view and couldn't share his summit joy with others. Alberto had such a short euphoric moment at the top of K2. Time was running out. He needed to quickly go down again, to reach Camp 3 before dark.

While climbing down the summit track, Alberto finally met Little Pasang, who handed over his camera. He took some selfies. [155] Next, Alberto would meet Lars and then Cecilia.

---

[155] http://dogayakacis.com/2014/04/29/2008-k2-faciasi/

Forty-two

The Korean team climbers were heading toward the summit, so Alberto met them also.

In his eyes, time was everything, but they had pressed their luck. The sun was still overhead, but it was inclining into the west. It was 4.45pm and it would be dark by around 8pm.

He also met Pemba, Gerard, and then Chhiring. Before saying "Goodbye!" to each other, Chhiring photographed Alberto.

When Alberto met Hugues and Karim, he realized they had a long way to go. Alberto especially worried about Hugues' climb.

'Hang on, this doesn't look good,' he said himself. 'Continuing to the top? The summit's still a long way from here. It'll take you two to three hours more.[156] And, then, descending... in darkness?'

In his eye, they were insane. They were taking a big gamble!

Meanwhile, Little Pasang finally stood on the summit at 5.15pm. The next climber was Lars at 5.30pm. He became the first Norwegian to summit K2. Lars and Little Pasang shared the summit joy, and took several shots of each other by exchanging cameras.[157] Then, Cecilia showed up at the other end of the summit ridge. She reached the top of K2 at 5.45pm.

Jumic climbed onto the summit ridge. He was going to wait for his teammates before putting his ice ax firmly down there. Next were Kim, and Park. Behind them was Go. She was climbing up toward the ridge. And Hwang was behind her. When Lars took one more shot of the Korean group, Kim had joined Jumic. Below him were Park, Go and Hwang. Little Kim wasn't in the group.

As soon as Go reached the ridge, the team quickly regrouped. The last-ditch efforts for Go's summit were assigned to Hwang and Jumic, after Kim and Park left for the summit.

---

[156] *See* p. 121 in this book.

[157] http://www.thesummitk2.com/#filter=.climbers,+.menu

Go was exhausted. Hwang was at her front and Jumic following behind. She had taken off her oxygen mask. It had probably became useless, having run out of oxygen. But she was still shouldering her backpack. Hwang and Jumic were still dependent on their oxygen.

It was the final assault, but she was struggling. Her pace was getting slower. She stopped often to catch her breath. The climbers' shadows cast by the sun went long toward the east side.

When she rested again at the middle of the ridge, Hwang headed toward the summit as if on a mission. Jumic was still guarding her closely from behind, though the summit was almost within reach.

While Park and Little Pasang had taken photos, Kim had been shooting his video camera to make Go's K2 summit footage. She was struggling hard and just one step from glory.

As soon as Go finally reached to the summit, she flopped down beside Kim. Jumic also reached the summit. It was almost 6pm.

The summit was the dome-shaped and wide. All of them took off their oxygen backpacks. They didn't need supplementary oxygen.

Cecilia was still there. She approached Go to congratulate her. Go was using a bottle of emergency oxygen to catch her breath. They shared summit ecstasy and then posed together for photos. It was a rare event for two women to be stood on the K2 summit. Go held the Norwegian flag in her hand when Lars took shots.

She took more photos with Kim and the Kolon Sport flag.[158] Then she shared her success with her sponsor by satellite call.

"Thanks to all," Go said, sharing her joy with other colleagues. "Fighting!" She shouted.

The next wave toward the summit was the Norit climbers. Pemba was the first. He reached the summit around 6.15pm. Chhiring was on the summit ridge and could see the climbers who had summited. Pemba was talking with a Sherpa.[159] Cecilia and Lars were gazing down the beauty of the scenery, and just about to start their descent. Kim was shouldering his backpack, kneeling down. He was surrounded by his team members. Were they talking about their descent plan?

Gerard had reached the summit around 6.25pm. His dream to be the first Irish person to reach K2 summit had come true. Pemba welcomed him

---

[158] http://www.kolonsport.com/komiyoung/date/photo05/pop_
photo09.html

[159] http://abcnews.go.com/Nightline/k2-deadliest-day/story?id=11358828

warmly. After taking a rest, Gerard lifted the Irish flag over his head.[160] It was a euphoric moment for the climbers, who grinned ecstatically. Chhiring arrived on the summit at 6.36pm and radioed the news to his Camp 4 colleagues. His summit was symbolically the triumphant achievement of the American International team.

---

[160] http://abcnews.go.com/Nightline/photos/climbers-fall-death-attempting -k2-11361962/image-11362209

Forty-three

Cas reached the summit behind Chhiring. He made some video footage of Pemba and Gerard.

When Cas turned back toward the summit ridge, two climbers had almost reached the end of the ridge. One of them was Wilco. Cas took a photo of him. It was 6.37pm.

If we look at the photograph more closely, there was one more climber, Little Kim. [161] He had dramatically turned up behind Wilco! It was great come-from-behind. Even his teammates thought that Little Kim would not make it. But he didn't throw in the towel. It was only through sheer willpower that he could make that summit ridge. His dream became a step closer.

Wilco and Little Kim were making slow progress. Behind them, Karim and Hugues were also climbing. The summited climbers were worried about their late descent, but couldn't contemplate abandoning these last climbers who were coming from the summit ridge to bag their crowns.

"Go, Wilco!"

"Go, Little Kim!"

For the summited climbers, waiting fifteen to twenty minutes was not a short time. It was killing them. Wasting precious time was the first thing they encountered as the price of a summit. The sun was sinking fast. Seeing and filming the sunset on K2 summit was such a gorgeous reward. The twilight was so beautiful.

The sun had set by the time Little Kim finally made it to the top. His team couldn't delay any further. Little Kim should descend immediately. He might not have enough time to recover from exhaustion.

It was almost 7pm. Chhiring had already gone down as soon as he made his brief summit footage. Pemba was also thinking to get out as soon as possible but Wilco had not made it, yet. The last waves rolling onto the K2 summit were Karim, Hugues and Wilco. Gerard wanted to share his

---

[161] p. 104-5, *Surviving K2* by Wilco Van Rooijen

summit joy with his partner Annie, who had waited for summit news in Alaska. After finishing his talk with her, he handed his satellite phone and camera to Pemba.

At 7pm, Karim arrived at the summit, greatly exhausted. He took off his backpack and planted his ice ax onto it. Hugues and Wilco arrived on the summit at 7.10pm. [162] As soon as Wilco got his breath back, Gerard and Pemba hugged him.[163] It was the wildest moment in their dreams and had taken a year of training. They were all giddy.

While the Norit climbers were enjoying their summit joy, Hugues made a satellite call home.

"It's minus twenty degrees, I'm at 8611 meters. I'm too cold, I'm too happy. Thank you."

The dominant issue now was the shadow of the K2 pyramid. It had expanded longer over the China side. As the color of sunset became darker, it became a danger sign. As soon as the twilight was over, it would fade to black. They knew the darkness was near.

Hugues and Karim got off the summit while Wilco was making a satellite call to Maarten of NLBC, according to his protocol.

"Maarten, we're on the summit of K2!" Wilco spoke. "Gerard, Cas, Pemba and myself. Over. At 6 o'clock local time. Over. I named him, didn't I?" Wilco spoke.

"   . . . "

"Gerard, Pemba, Cas and myself. It was a very tough job, but I'll tell you all about it later on," Wilco spoke again.

Wilco's ceremony took ages. The cold had bitten into the climbers. Pemba realized that he was in a summit trap. He had to get out of it, immediately. As soon as he grabbed his backpack, he started to move downward, slowly.[164] Wilco was still talking on the phone with Maarten.

"I've never been on such a hard climb. Particularly from a logistic point of view."

---

[162] https://www.flickr.com/photos/25037111@N07/2904790733/in/photostream/

[163] http://abcnews.go.com/Nightline/photos/climbers-fall-death-attempting-k2-11361962/image-11362191

[164] http://www.businessinsider.com.au/the-summit-2008-k2-tragedy-2013-10#the-dutch-team-including-leader-wilco-van-rooijen-cas-van-de-gevel-ger-mcdonnell-the-first-irishman-to-summit-k2-and-pemba-gyalje-reached-the-top-around-7-pm-30

Wind swirled across the summit and the ridge. It was increasingly cold. Gerard, who was wearing his gloves started to descend a few steps behind Pemba.

Then, surprisingly, one more climber was coming up. It was Marco! Pemba and Gerard had passed him when they went down.

Marco was now climbing toward K2 summit from the other end of the summit ridge. He was worn out. When Wilco was about to pass, Marco sat on his knees on the footprinted ridge. Wilco ignored him. When Cas tried to pass Marco, he saw Marco's body language begging something. Cas stopped to help him quickly. It was 7.30pm.

In his sitting position, Marco had to wear his outer vest with the various sponsors' logos and then held up his ski-stick with various flags. Cas photographed him several times.[165] Since the evening sun's flare had disappeared, he had to use a flash.[166]

After finishing the photo session, Marco took out his satellite phone, and started to punch the button pad so he could tell his main sponsor of his achievement. It was just before dark. Cas couldn't be with him any longer.

On that day, 18 climbers summited the top of K2. Marco was the last climber, left alone in the darkness.

---

[165] http://www.altarezianews.it/2008/10/28/marco-confortola-quei-giorni-sul-k2/
[166] http://www.laprovinciadisondrio.it/stories/Cronaca/212130_confortolain_cima_alk2_in_un_libro_laltra_verit/

Forty-four

Yes! Every camp in K2 Base Camp had crackled with loud enthusiasm for a while, hearing the summit news. K2BC colleagues cheered and were elated by their teams' achievements.

It was well-known on K2, though, that footing on the summit didn't mean the summiteers' mission was accomplished. Nobody knew what would happen during the climbers' descents. That was tough on all the big mountains. The perfect victory would be safely returning to K2 Base Camp. Since the mountain had changed from light to dark, the primary concern of each camp was their climbers' safe return to Camp 4.

The more the darkness deepened, the more people in K2 Base Camp worried. There was nothing they could do. Just... kept calm and wait. However, hopes of the climbers' return to Camp 4 were slowly fading. No news from the mountain was not good news.

There were nail-biting moments. Roeland, the manager of Norit base camp, had heard radio communications from the Korean camp before midnight.

'What's going on?'

August 2, D+1

It was around 1am. A radio crackled in Norit's basecamp, calling urgently:

"Roeland, Roeland!"

It was Cas. And Roeland sensed that a something unknown was coming.

"DISASTER!"

Roeland couldn't do anything. So, he decided to head down to the Korean camp. The Korean team had the most powerful radio base station with the highest antenna.

When Roeland got to the Korean mess tent, there was panic. Several people were present, including Lee the ex-lawyer and the oldest in the team, woman climber Song, Captain Azeem the team's liaison officer and the Nepali cook Ngawang. Lee had climbed to Camp 2 with Team 2, but he had given up at that point.

Not long after, Chris K of the American International team joined the Korean camp at K2BC. He had climbed all the way down the Abruzzi route from Camp 4 to K2BC, arriving around midnight.

The K2BC people eagerly awaited more news from the mountain. The Korean team radioed in news on their situation but Roeland and Chris couldn't understand.

Only sporadic radio communications in Korean signaled that something was happening on the mountain. They could feel the Korean team members were in pain.

Around 2am, another communication came through. This time, it was a burst of rapid-fire speech in a hysterical tone. The team members' faces hardened to stone. One of the Koreans stood quietly away from the group, weeping.

Forty-five

At 3.30am, Roeland received a call from Maarten of NLBC. He said he had a satellite call from Wilco saying that Marco, Gerard and he were bivvying over the Traverse during the night. Roeland and Chris returned to Norit's mess tent around 4am.

By receiving more radio calls from Camp 4, K2BC people could figure out that eight climbers had succeeded in returning to Camp 4, but the status of ten climbers was uncertain.

They might be Wilco, Gerard, Marco, Hugues, Karim, Rolf, Jumic, Hwang, Little Kim and Park.

'Did K2 trap them? Who can help them now?'

As the sun was rising, those who had news of the disaster gathered in K2BC. They looked at the mountain up above them. It was frustrating to think of the rescue itself. K2 was high.

"It's a big mountain. It would take at least two days climb to reach Camp 4," someone said.

"How about the weather? The fates of the climbers hang on themselves?" said another climber.

"How the effort for search and rescue is going on up there?"

A little later, they heard from Camp 4 by radio that a Korean rescue team was on the way.[167][168] K2BC asked the Singaporean team at Camp 3 to remain on standby. The team put off their descent, and started to monitor radios while snow and ice melted.

Later, K2BC people received news from Camp 4 that some of the climbers were descending to the lower camps because of the worsening weather conditions. This meant missing climbers were at risk of losing potential manpower.

At 12.10pm K2BC time, NLBC updated its blog.

---

[167] *See* 8am situation on the back-cover photograph.
[168] *See* 10am situation in p. 121 of this book.

Status as far as we know
"K2BC can see six people standing still in the Bottleneck. Two Haps are on their way up..."

This was re-blogged by Pat Falvey, an Irish mountain climber and a friend of Gerard. He might have checked all K2BC blogs in Ireland concerned to find out Gerard's status. In the meantime, EverestNews.com made a correction on the number.

"One unconfirmed report states as many as 7 climbers could be seen up high..."

It was seven, not six. And then, EverestNews.com updated its blog again:

"Things are real bad on K2. The Koreans, we are told, are sending their Sherpas up to try to rescue climbers. What remains of the Dutch teams at camp 4 is expected to go up with a couple of others."

In Islamabad, the Pakistani Ministry of Tourism had an emergency meeting at 3pm with the travel agencies concerned. The head of the ministry had called them.

After the meeting, each travel agency sent the "Help one another!" message to their staff and Haps in K2BC. Asghar Ali Porik, the owner of Jasmine Tours, collected all the available information on the climbers' status and relayed it through EverestNews.com:

"Jasmine Tours has Norit K2 Expedition, Sunny Mountain Chogori Expedition and International K2 Expedition (the Jamine Tours International K2 expedition).
It's learnt that three of its Norit K2 expedition members are above bottleneck.
Sunny Mountain Chogori Expedition all members are safe and helping the rescue efforts.
Hosilito Bite is coming down towards BC.
Blue Sky Trek and Tours has Korean Expedition and it is told that their two Korean members and one Nepali Sherpa is above bottleneck. The fellow Koreans are helping in rescue effort from C4.

Nazir Sabir Expedition has a Serbian K2 Expedition and yesterday their one Serbian member Mr. Mandic fell down... and rest of the members are heading down to base camp.

Adventure Tours Pakistan had an American expedition all members are safe, however high altitude porter died while helping in the rescue effort. It is told that ATP one French member is missing.

Hunza Guides Pakistan has a Singaporean K2 expedition, it is told that they are at C3 and helping other climbers in rescue efforts.

Hushe Trek and Tours has Italian K2 expedition and it is told that their one members is hurt near C4 and HP with this climber is bring him down to base camp the other member is safe at base camp."

But still a big question remained:

"What's going on up at the mountain?"

The hours drifted by with a discontinuity of news from Camp 4. By 5pm, the only news from Camp 4 was that Marco had made it back alive. He'd said two Sherpas helped him down.

Two Sherpas? This news came from the updated Norit blog. But no one knew exactly how Marco had made it back to Camp 4. And no one heard the whereabouts of Wilco, Gerard, Hugues, Karim and the Korean team climbers who had failed to return to Camp 4.

Around that time, Nick and Jelle touched down at the bottom of the Cesen route, and were met by the Serb Hoselito there. They heard the news of the missing climbers. Wild rumors were swirling over the disaster-struck K2BC:

"Except for Pemba and Cas, all climbers are still trapped in the bottleneck."

"Nine climbers are dead."

Forty-six

"Many think others are missing . . . Alberto Zerain, one of the first to summit and is now down and calling in reports, reports several dead and 6 missing: Of the several dead: 2 Pakistanis, 1 Serbian, others withheld... THINGS ARE VERY BAD ON K2..."

This news was reported by EverestNews.com, after sunset.
Alberto? This might have been the first reaction from the K2 climbers. Lars the Norwegian climber would testify, four or five years later, that:

"Alberto was kinds of a mythical figure. So I didn't see Alberto close up at all until I met him when he was on his way down."[169]

In fact, most of the K2BC people never heard the name before the EverestNews.com news, and they knew so little about him. Yeah, he was one of the mysterious climbers during the 2008 K2 season.

"The basecamp is now a funeral," said Alberto, according to the Spanish news site Gara.com.

A funeral? Exactly! Climbing K2 had been a matter of life and death. Just who was Alberto?

Alberto Zerain, the Basque climber, was originally a member of Spanish Broad Peak Expedition, made up as follows: [170]

1. Javier Compos Duaso (L) (40)
2. Juan Carlos Gonzalez (56)
3. Dieo Hernandez Garcia (26)
4. Santiago Martin Corrales (44)
5. Rafael Merchan Cotos (50)

---

[169] *The Summit*, a documentary film by Nick Ryan
[170] http://www.idazten.com/index.php?option=com_content&view =article&id=1245&catid=51

    6. Alfredo Garcia Pascual (26)
    7. Catalina Quesada Castro (39)
    8. Aitor Las Hayas Madariaga (47)
    9. Aberto Zerain Berasategui (48)

So, Alberto had challenged the 8056m giant Broad Peak, but his team became almost devastated by injuries and helicopter evacuations. The team leader had been replaced two times: from Javier Compos Duaso to Juan Carlos Gonzalez, and then to Santiago Martin Corrales.

Alberto had visited K2BC. After climbing K2 two times, he made his Broad Peak summit push with his colleagues. While climbers in other teams were finally successful in summiting Broad Peak after many ups and downs, his team failed. Alberto also had to give up climbing due to a lack of acclimatization and the consequent headaches.

After that, Alberto might have thought Broad Peak wasn't the right mountain for him. Broad Peak was also crowded. But there was one he could gain. He couldn't avoid his eye settling on K2. He got acclimatized.

How could he make it possible to climb K2? First, he saw a big hole in the K2 wall. He had found an officer of the French International Expedition had fallen ill with lung edema and was evacuated to the military camp at Concordia on June 22.

'Hmmm, no liaison officer in the team!'

He saw it as a big loophole in K2 security. If K2 security had failed, everything might be possible for non-K2 climbers. As long as the loophole remained in a vacuum, greedy climbers would flow in continually from nearby mountains. This loophole in K2 would be abused by many climbers. Alberto was the first among many.

He needed some information to understand K2, but it was also an easy matter to get it from K2 blogs.

On July 9, Alberto made his first visit to the French International team in K2BC with the help of his Spanish colleagues, including a woman called Lina. Alberto carried a big backpack.

His hosts Hugues and Nick were friendly, but they had nothing to do with the business of the Abruzzi route. Alberto found that Wilco was notorious for piggybacking, and he would charge a fee as far as the Cesen route was concerned. It was a logical step for him to get on the Abruzzi route. Other trial climbers had the same result.

The Abruzzi route has been loosely dominated by the Korean and Serbian teams. K2's mood was buoyant following the early cooperating meeting. In it, Alberto could make progress over to Camp 2 without any problem.

For the sleepovers at the high camps, he would have needed shelter. Probably, his savior was Shaheen the Haps' leader in the Serbian team. The offer was probably negotiable.

Obviously, Abruzzi climbers might be bothered by this upstart and with the negotiation. Mike Farris, the leader of the American International team, and Milivoj Erdeljan, the member of Serbian team, weren't quiet about piggyback climbers. Others might have thought that eventually, most of the non-K2 climbers would go away because of the long period of bad weather.

However, Alberto was exceptional. He never gave up his K2 ambition. Broad Peak was in bad shape that year with snow and ice melting higher up than normal.[171] This had made the rockfall hazard severe, while K2 was looking to be in better shape.

All the circumstances were set up in his favor, compared with his previous K2 attempts in 1996 on the Cesen route and in 2006. How much money and time had he invested in challenging K2 so far? He'd had a perfect acclimatization by attempting Broad Peak. Because his teammates had evacuated, food and gas were plentiful to endure through the crappy weather.

When the good weather forecast finally came, Alberto also wanted to get acquainted with K2BC's climbing plans, in order to make his own strategies and movements.

Around lunch time on July 25, he visited the K2 French International team again with Lina and a Spaniard, probably Aitor. He returned to his camp empty-handed, but couldn't get to sleep.

'They have a date. I need to know the meeting result for my planning.'

So, Alberto sent an invitation to the K2 French International team members. The next day, the invited K2 climbers came down to the Broad Peak Spanish basecamp. The food was delicious, with a Spanish flavor. But there was no free lunch. There was a purpose behind the lunch invitation. While eating and drinking, Alberto was listening and absorbing every word. He would capitalize on the information for his K2 challenge.

For his summit push, Alberto went to K2BC on July 28. Aitor and Lina accompanied him. K2BC had no wall and was empty, since it was the day when the Abruzzi Korean Team 2 climbers had started their summit push early in the morning.

---

[171] http://myhimalayas.wordpress.com/category/week-in-review/page/18/

So could they make free access as they liked? At first, the Spaniards slipped up inside the Serbian camp. Finding it uncomfortable with the Serb leader and the Pakistani liaison officer, Alberto had to change his plan and went into Hugues' tent for the night.

On July 29, he started his summit push alone. When the Korean Team 2 climbers arrived at Camp 2 in the late afternoon for a night's rest, Alberto also arrived to Camp 2. Alberto had planned daily radio contact with his Broad Peak colleague through a certain frequency and at a certain time. At 5pm, he made a radio contact with Aitor.

"I am ok in Camp 2, roger," Alberto said.

"Received, tomorrow we return to communicate at the same time, good afternoon," Aitor quickly replied.

There, he met Shaheen who was sick. Alberto had to stay one more day at Camp 2. His climbing schedule was also thwarted by the delay of the upper climbers.

At 5pm, July 30, he got bounced back and turned on his radio to communicate with Aitor.

"Aitor, I'm still here in Camp 2 by blizzard and you okay?" Alberto asked.

"We're also in Camp 2 (Broad Peak), good thing is to save battery power, tomorrow we talk," Aitor replied.

Next day (July 31), Alberto started his climb toward Camp 3. It was a fine day. When he arrived at Camp 3, the Norwegian couple Cecilia and Rolf was still there.

It was 5pm. Lonely, scared to lose his language, he radioed to Aitor but there was no reply. He thought his battery had gone flat. After saying "Hello and good-bye", he abandoned it.

He might have had several reasons for not joining the summit plan with Team 2. First, he didn't have enough food and gas since he had wasted a day at Camp 2. Second, he was tired and bored. He had to move on. Alberto's summit strategy was simple, and brilliant. It was 'hit-and-run'. It meant that he would 'join the summit group to use their logistics, and after topping out K2 summit, make it to Camp 3 as quickly as possible'.

Alberto had a good early nap before hitting the slope for his final summit push. The great guide rail was the highway. He could reach Camp 4 around midnight. His expectation was the Camp 4 climbers were already on the way toward the bottleneck, but he was wrong.

He confronted Pemba there. Eventually, he could be a latent climbing force but his gut instinct was not to stay in the group. He didn't belong.

When the rope came after a long wait, he snapped it up and devoured its yield.

How did his climb affect others? Nobody has yet explained it, for some reason.

After the K2 top out, and when he was descending past all the climbers, he caught up Øystein at the Bottleneck. When he had passed Camp 4, one of its climbers had a cup of tea outside his tent.[172] Alberto desperately needed to have a sip of it but the Camp 4 climber, probably Eric, didn't care for him. When he got down to Camp 3 it was late. But he was glad to find that the Serbian team's Haps were there. Alberto heard about the disaster and realized it was deepening.

The next morning, he heard about the disaster from the Singaporean team as well. But he decided to go down. Did he regard the disaster as irrelevant to him? When he passed K2BC, no one congratulated him. He might think that K2BC was like a graveyard.

He ran on down to his Broad Peak basecamp.

---

[172] p. 68, *No Way Down* by Graham Bowley

Forty-seven

Climbing K2 is not easy, but it was open to experienced climbers. Of course, with that comes responsibilities.

The chief controversy in Alberto's K2 blitz was whether he had obtained a K2 permit or not. If not, he was not a fair player. Obviously, his colleagues Aitor and Lina didn't have K2 permits. It is fairly certain, if questioned, he would have responded:

"Yes, I did! From the first moment, I had a BP & K2 doubleheader plan."

However, it would not have meant he had already secured a K2 permit *before* his challenge of K2.

In the 2008 season at Karakorum, the Spanish expeditions were everywhere. They were the dominating figures in the 2008 Karakorum as below: [173]

> Spanish Broad Peak Expedition
> Spanish G–I, G–II Expedition
> Spanish G–II Expedition
> French / Spanish Broad Peak Expedition
> Spanish G–IV Expedition
> Spanish Lotak–III Expedition
> Spanish Rakaposhi Expedition
> Spanish G–I & G–II Expedition

Among the many Spanish climbers was one more who had been serious in challenging K2. Jorge Egocheaga had visited Broad Peak on July 10–11 and K2BC on July 12. He climbed K2 around July 19, and Nick Rice had noticed Jorge's claim for his climbing achievement of reaching beyond Camp 4 on the Abruzzi route.

---

[173] http://www.k2climb.net/page/2008.htm

Who was Jorge and where did he come from? He was one of the well-known climbers in the Himalayan circle. He led the 2008 Spanish G–II Expedition. Its team members were:

Jorge Egocheaga (L)	M	42	Spanish
Joelle Brupbacher	F	30	Swiss
Martin Ramos Garcia	M	41	Espanola
Miguel Angel Perez Alvarez	M	49	Spanish
Rafael Garcia Belderrain	M	38	Spanish
Alberto Zerain Berasategui	M	48	Spanish

Alberto was also one of the team members of this 2008 Spanish G–II Expedition. Considering this information, we can figure out several points.

First, there was a close connection between Alberto and Jorge. It would not be surprising if we say that Jorge's K2 climb might have been helped by the Spanish Broad Peak expedition, especially Alberto. Second, did Jorge have a K2 permit? If the answer was "unlikely!", then his K2 climb using the fixed ropes was unlawful, strictly speaking. Third, Alberto surely had a doubleheader plan. However, wasn't it Broad Peak–GII, instead of Broad Peak–K2?

If he insists he had a K2 plan as well, then, a question pops up: Did he hold three permits for BP–GII–K2 before his challenge of K2?

Of course, it's possible he could have changed his mind later into a K2 instead of a GII plan. But again a question pops up: Had he secured his K2 permit alone and before his K2 challenge?

Though many then-K2 climbers believed that Alberto was a stranger, most of his friends believed him that he had obtained a K2 permit. Sure, his friends had to trust his words. But had Alberto acquired the permit *before* his K2 climb?

In the letter written by Captain Muhammad Anwar Sharif, the liaison officer of the Broad Peak Spanish team, he mentioned Alberto's K2 challenge:

> "After 12 days bad weather our expedition members decided to go to camp 2 on 29 July 2008, 30 July to camp 3 of Broad Peak.
> Among the 6 members one member Alberto Zerrain had permit of K2 as well, he preferred climbing K2 than Broad Peak because he had left with very short time of five days.

He asked me about his intentions after consulting with all members we saw him off for K2 on 28 July 2008."[174]

Was it true that he had the K2 permit before his K2 climb? Did the officer see it? Or had Alberto and the liaison officer ignored the rule of law?

If this was the case, we can't resist questioning the permit issuance system.

Of course, issuing permits is none of a liaison officer's concern. Permit issuance is the sovereign practice of the concerned country, in this case the Pakistani Ministry of Tourism.

It carries an enormous responsibility. So, the Pakistani government has attached a liaison officer to each expedition to protect the territory and climbers by overseeing and administrating the process. And it means, the liaison officer has controlled all unlawful practices. The existence of the liaison officers was to protect the best interests of the climbers by exercising law and order diligently. Then, there wouldn't have been any territory violation.

Traditionally, the authorities have issued permits in advance of trekking.[175] This system has been relaxed in various ways. Nowadays, compared with the past, individual climbers can obtain permits on the spot.

Thus, with the unfolding 2008 K2 disaster, some questions arose about the business of permits. Were there any issuances of permits *after* climbing? Hasn't the culture of risk-taking combined with or degraded into a money matter? If the opportunity arises, haven't climbers tried to summit their preferred mountain? Have these kinds of practices become the new normal because the authorities can make extra money?

For example, after summiting K2, climbers liked to bag Broad Peak. It would not be their rope, but the rope already fixed by other expeditions. The other way around: if a climber summited Broad Peak successfully, he would have rushed to K2 to try his luck.

These kinds of doubleheader games have been normal since Broad Peak and K2 are neighboring mountains. Capable climbers have grabbed their glories. Of course, the less-capable climbers can also try it, but a K2–Broad Peak doubleheader was a greedy and dangerous bid. Although it was an end-of-season occurrence, taking on two mountains was not easy since the climber's strength was already exhausted by summiting one.

---

[174] *See* the comment on http://www.alpinist.com/doc/web08x/newswire-letter-nazir-sabir

[175] http://www.alpineclub.org.pk/mount_rules.shtml

Forty-eight

In the 2008 K2 season, K2 was crowded from the beginning. Because of the Tibetan issue with the 2008 Beijing Olympic Games, unfortunately no foreign climbers were allowed to climb Everest in that spring season. So many climbers switched their climb to the mountains in Karakorum. Was there an excessive issuance of permits?

The inside story of the promiscuous permit business looks complicated and never ending—beyond the scope of my interest and probably no one will get to the bottom of it.

Getting back to the issue of Alberto's involvement in the 2008 K2 disaster, let's think for a moment about the location of the base camp for the Spanish Broad Peak Expedition. The expedition set up its base camp at the half-way point between Broad Peak and K2. Why? The main purpose of the expedition was obviously the challenge for Broad Peak. But weren't their eyes on K2? Wasn't this an ideal and ambitious location to strike for Broad Peak, K2, and GII, if necessary?

On August 2, Aitor's satellite phone interview popped up on Youtube.[176] After summiting K2, the asserted permit holder Alberto came back to his Broad Peak base camp. There, he reported his glory by emails. And he started many interviews with Spanish media about his achievement and the disaster on August 2,[177] August 3[178] and August 4.[179] Some footage showed photographs of Alberto with sponsors' logos including a banner titled "Broad Peak–K2 expedition".

On August 4, Alberto was hurriedly trekking down to Skardu, while the K2 disaster heated up as the world's headline news.

---

[176] www.youtube.com/watch?v=PmxD9W6TLUI

[177] www.youtube.com/watch?v=C-yFA-I4-ao

[178] www.youtube.com/watch?v=Odm_iCR2qcM

[179] www.youtube.com/watch?v=tt4yi3lbevM

Fortunately or unfortunately, he was in the global spotlight later, from the media to the climbing world. Many praised him as "Superb, Alberto!":

"Alberto did all the trail breaking."

"He was only one to get there and descend on time."

"He has only person who had the perfect day."

"He was the climber among climbers."

Sure, he had wowed them that disastrous day, but his performance was not flawless.

Finding Alberto in the K2 Bottleneck gave the climbers a jolt. And Wilco, who led the Norit team's expedition, didn't hesitate to criticize him. Wilco was insistent.

"I and the others were astonished to find Zerain already there, directing the route setting," he said. "We had discussed this so many times, what had to be done and who had to take care of this job."

Later, in his book, Wilco pointed out that Alberto's climb was purely a piggyback ride:

"He has dependent his climbing with other team's logistic."

In another place, he also discussed the painful rope-fixing works:

> "Bring up those ropes to 8,000 meter, it's a hell of a job. The first four till five weeks, every day fixing the ropes 100 meter by 100 meter by 100 meter, and then going back just by the rope, you know, going down to the base camp." [180]

The Serbian team also criticized these kinds of rule breaking climbers.

> "They joined the line by their own will, without agreement." [181]

Against all those criticisms, Alberto himself argued that:

> "I shared my cheese and pasta with the Haps. [182] I did rope-fixing works with them."
>
> "On the summit day, I fixed ropes as the lead climber in the Bottleneck. I contibuted my ice-screws as well. I did the trail-breaking works alone."
>
> "The Korean team leader Kim said to me "Thank you!""

---

[180] *The Summit*, a documentary film by Nick Ryan

[181] p 3, *2008 K2 Serbian Report* by Milivoj Erdeljan.

[182] p. 63, *No Way Down* by Graham Bowley

In his report, Alberto also claimed that he was a "solo climber". However, was Alberto a real solo climber to climb K2? Has anyone ever climbed the top of the notorious K2 solo? No, not one single person has done that!

In addition, he couldn't continue his climb in the Bottleneck without other climbers' help in supplying the ropes. Most of the other parts of the climbers' work was given away to him without the climbers' consents.

So, Alberto's solo claim was appalling and absurd.

Then, what are the implications of his K2 climb? First, wasn't Alberto's K2 glory stolen? And second, wasn't his K2 success linked to the disaster unfolding behind him and to the climbers' deaths?

Questions about Alberto's K2 climb would never stop.

Forty-nine

August 2, D+1, Saturday afternoon

"Find Wilco!"

It was the message given to K2 Base Camp people. Since then, Chris and several people had been peering through a telescope to find Wilco.[183] It was around 5.45pm when Chris spotted an orange dot through the telescope. The dot climber was out of route high near the Shoulder on the far left of the Cesen route. Since it was orange, the dot climber seemed like Wilco. But K2BC climbers couldn't confirm it, yet.

At 6.30pm, Norit K2BC tried to call Gerard by satellite phone. Surprisingly, the climber who answered the call was Pemba at Camp 4. Roeland urged him:

"Get a climber who looks like Wilco moving toward the Cesen route between Shoulder and Camp 3."[184]

Around 8pm, Pemba finally started his descent from Camp 4. When it became dark, he had to use his headlamp. Cas also followed him. But he had a problem. When he had to change batteries on his headlamp, he dropped a battery into the void!

Pemba reached Camp 3 without finding Wilco. He was exhausted. He went to sleep in a tent, while Cas faced an unexpected open bivvy somewhere on the route, without light. Wilco also was sleeping somewhere off the route without shelter. Spending a second night on the mountain would reduce his chances of survival.

On the evening news of the day, a Pakistani TV station ARY reported:

"Those who perished included South Koreans and Nepalese. Serbian, Norwegian, Dutch and French climbers were also

---

[183] www.youtube.com/watch?v=3oGkvjUlTls

[184] http://www.everestnews.com/pak2008/k22008sadnews080520080101.htm

believed to be among those who might have died. Other climbers are feared to be missing."

The news of the K2 disaster was filtering out in the various ways to media machines, and vague accounts were trickling out of K2.

The K2 news also had gone down from high camp to a media machine. In Europe, a large story with the headline "Swedish Climber In Death Drama" began to pop up in European online news services.

> "Upon learning of the avalanche, Strang team broke off its ascent and went to help another group to safety after one of its members had been killed.
>
> As they climbed down, another climber lost his life and Strang almost went down with him, according the climber's spokesperson, Joachim von Stedingk.
>
> Speaking to TT, von Stedingk explained that as Strang was preparing for a second attempt to reach the summit, parts of the ice wall called Bottleneck Couloir slammed down.
>
> "This avalanche caused a further two deaths and at least eight people are completely cut off now. How they will come down now nobody knows."
>
> Right now, his team is climbing down to a lower level with injured and shocked climbers.
>
> The teams are presently at 7500 metres, which significantly worsens rescue services' chances of helping them."

It was at 13:42 Central Europe Time. Very fast! And the news was posted by Claudia Rodas for Swedish news agency TT. Of course, the original source of the news was Swedish Fred Strang.

It was the story of high mountains. He reported *parts of the ice wall and the avalanche* as the cause of the deaths. Did he see it? Did he witness the deaths? By the way, where did he report the news? Wasn't 7500 meters somewhere between Camp 4 (7700m) and Camp 3 (7400m)? Then, what time did Fred's group go down from Camp 4 to Camp 3? These questions have huge implications, and we will come back these matters, later. Anyway, Fred must be a great storyteller, and he knew how to make news while others were in stress and distress with many questions about the deaths and the unfolding events.

While the disaster was leaking out in that way, Fred's group was continuing their descent from Camp 3 all the way down to K2 Base Camp.

The K2 disaster was breaking news for frantic media, having a field day with it. The bad news was traveling fast. World newsrooms reported the K2 disaster as A-class news. It was sending shock waves around the globe. However, high confusion and complexity was reigning in the news, and some flawed reporting was adding to the confusion and the disaster's woes.

Until now, the main news sources about K2 was the Norit blog. But no more. Explorersweb (ExWeb), a news service that tracks climbing expeditions, also reported and updated the K2 progress with: K2 Saturday wrap-up of events.[185] The frustrated families and friends were flooding helplines in a desperate bid for more information on their loved ones, while the public eye was on the TV news.

In America, the morning and afternoon news would present another example of news organizations frantically reporting information under competitive pressure.

What happened to the climbers during the day and night?

When Nick updated his dispatch, an American news agency picked him up as the voice of K2BC. His satellite phone voice was aired. He considered the survivors had a chance. So, he had not given up hope that the climbers could still be alive. He hoped for a miracle. Yes, a miracle could happen.[186]

---

[185] www.k2climb.net/news.php?id=17458—Unavailable, now.

[186] http://www.theguardian.com/sport/2008/aug/31/9

Fifty

August 3, D+2, Sunday

A new day dawned. It was around 5.15am when K2BC people spotted Wilco again. The Norit blog could run again through the mirror site provided by ExWeb. Meanwhile, there was a report from the American International team:

"We all eight are safely back in base camp."[187]

Fred started to again call his PR agent Joachim von Stedingk to report the disastrous K2 events.

Unsubstantiated rumors of the grim news continued to run wildly. On top of the wild rumors, as usual, Hollywood-style fairy tales were starting to pass around the globe. One story would lead to another. All the climbers had a story to tell. Their turnaround or stories of survival were big news. The most popular was the one about Fred's scoop.

Meantime, good news came from the mountain.

"Found Wilco!"

He was now at Camp 3 with Pemba and Cas.[188] After drinking water and hot tea, they made radio contact with K2BC. Cas filmed it. [189]

> **Pemba** at Camp 3: "We had big problem with radio and battery before, but now is a 100% clear?"
> **Roeland** at K2BC: "100% clear. Over."
> **Pemba**: "Okay, now I give a radio for Wilco. You can talk with Wilco."
> **K2BC**: " . . . "

---

[187] http://www.everestnews.com/pak2008/k22008sadnews080720080101.htm

[188] https://www.flickr.com/photos/25037111@N07/2905620272/in/photostream/

[189] http://www.liveleak.com/view?i=831_1217791162

Pemba: "Do you copy that?"
Roeland: "Yes, I copy you."
Pemba: "Okay, now Wilco is going to talk with you."
Wilco: "A quick update. We've just reached Camp 3. Everything is in good shape, except our feet. That's not surprising if you have to survive only on eating snow for three days. But we've got some bigger problems now. There are some people missing and we've seen some dead people, too." "Pemba wants to know more about that. Did you copy that? Over."
Roeland: "Yes, Wilco. Unfortunately, we're listening to you with tears in our eyes. We're grateful that you're safe. And we're going to do our best to get you down safely. Over."
Wilco: "Thanks. That's good to hear. If you walk around alone on this mountain for a few days . . . especially during a white-out, you would become very small." "I'm going to hand Pemba over to you. He wants to know more about Hugues. Over."[190]

Wilco was safe now. However, the status of other climbers was still unknown? The doctor, Eric, urged Camp 3 climbers to come down immediately.

And EverestNews.com updated the news as follows:

> UPDATE: "Wilco has just been located in Camp 3! How he got to camp 3 without other knowing? Hopefully Wilco can tell others, where various climbers are..."

Everyone was waiting for more news. Then, Maarten posted on the status of the other climbers:

> "We keep track of people who we know were on the same route as the Norit K2 team . . . We almost do know nothing about the Abruzzi climbing expeditions."

Since the K2 media floodgate had opened, all the climbers and officials were prey to journalists. Mr Shahzad Qaiser, the head of the Ministry of Tourism said to the journalists at Islamabad:

---

[190] www.youtube.com/watch?v=KaHr1_5ujoM

"We cannot sit as a spectator to this."
"This accident is a very sad and disastrous event in our mountaineering history."

The Ministry of Tourism in Islamabad was considering having an official press conference.

For further understanding of the complexity and darkness of the disaster, the media sought experts' views. Experts were popping up everywhere. In an interview with the BBC, Britain's most celebrated mountaineer Sir Chris Bonnington, who lost his colleague Nick Escourt in an avalanche on K2's western side during his expedition in 1978, said:

"It's a very serious and very dangerous mountain.
"It's enormous, very high, incredibly steep and much further north than Everest which means it attracts notoriously bad weather.
"No matter which route you take it's a technically difficult climb, much harder than Everest. The weather can change incredibly quickly, and in recent years the storms have become more violent. People who have recently been there have told me that the snow conditions are also getting worse."

Reinhold Messner, the Italian climbing legend who first completed all 14 peaks taller than 8000m (26,250 feet), described:

"The situation is very critical."
"If they now to reach the other side of the mountain, the Chinese side where there is another expedition and if this expedition could have bared the way up to the summit, there is a chance for them to survive, otherwise I don't see they will be saved."

Chinese side? The legend feared for the disaster.

The news on the disaster started to appear in the morning papers. AFP had reported that nine climbers had died and three were missing.

On August 3, 2008, 18:00 GMT edition, Deutsche Presse-Agentur (dpa) had run a headline: Rescue under way for climbers on K2 as 11 feared dead (2nd Roundup). Ghulam Mohammed, owner of the Blue Sky Treks and Tours operator, told the paper:

"After the accident one Nepali member of the Korean expedition managed to descend to a camp but went back to help his colleague who was suffering from frostbite. On their way back, both slipped and fell into a crevasse."

Went back? A spokesperson for Nazir Sabir Expedition also said to the press:

"The body of Serbian climber Dren Mandic was found near camp three and was buried by fellow climbers."

How absurd and confusing the news was! A Pakistani army spokesman, Maj. Farooq Firoz, told Reuters:

"We can take a helicopter up there to drop medicines and supplies, but carrying out an operation is very difficult."

The Lede, the New York Times' breaking-news blog had started its online updates on "the K-2 Tragedy".
Meanwhile, Tina Sjogren the co-founder of ExWeb criticized: Dance for scoops and fame on people's graves. [191] The Swede, Fred, would come under attack from ExWeb. At the same time, Tom Sjogren the co-founder of ExWeb said in an interview:

"If there are any survivors up there, they are pretty much on their own."

He also said of the climbers near the summit of K2:

"It's very likely that these people are dead, but small miracles happen all the time in the mountains."

---

[191] 3 August 2008, ExplorersWeb

Fifty-one

Hopes were fading fast for the victims' families. The biggest concern of the media was to confirm how many were dead.

On August 2, in Europe, the media had already reported the number of casualties. The editor of EverestNews.com also mentioned this:

> "Four have been reported dead including the 2 who died going UP, from 2 or more sources on the Mountain to EverestNews.com."

Mohammed Akram the Deputy President of ATP said:

> "Until now, seven died. There is a word that nine died, but it was not confirmed yet."

However, ExWeb had posted on the K2 Saturday wrap-up of events:

> "Numbers of perished are stated as high as 7 in various international media, however only one fatal accident has so far been confirmed."

Reuters reported that five climbers were missing, and the AFP seven dead. Ghulam Mohammad, the owner of Blue Sky Tours and Travels, said:

> "Five members of the Korean team had died including two Nepalese climbers."

Agostino Da Polenza, the president of the Italian Ev-K2-CNR committee, said in an interview with SkyItalia Television:

> "According to the rumours from the . . . base camp, there should be nine people dead and four still missing."

Fred reiterated to Swedish TT news agency, "at least nine died." But after Wilco was found, some were speaking of "11 dead certain." Fred also featured in a radio interview saying: "It is likely that eleven died."

And then, about 2.35pm CET time, TT reported headlines: "K2 Mountain Drama Over: 11 Deaths".

> "I carried both the living and the dead down from the mountain. At one point I was terrified as a Pakistani Sherpa fell on my back with all his weight. I was in a panic that he would drag all of us down with him, and screamed for him to use his ice pick, but he lost hold of it and flew off a 300 meter precipice," Strang told TT.
>
> Strang seems pretty sure about the accident's cause. After a long spell of bad weather, conditions suddenly improved on Friday, which spurred a large number of climbers to make their way to the top at the same time. However, the weather soon turned again.
>
> "We felt that this wouldn't turn out well and we retreated. The accidents could have been prevented," Strang told TT. "These mountains attract more and more inexperienced and naïve people who completely rely on the resources that are there, Sherpas, oxygen gas and weather reports."
>
> "Frednik Strang is now safe at an altitude of 5100m."

The reporter was Claudia Rodas again, through PR agent Joachim von Stedingk.

Nazir Sabir Expedition reported nine climbers were feared to have died and three others were missing. Deutsche Presse-Agentur quoted the words of retired Brigadier Mohammed Akram, spokesman for the Alpine Club of Pakistan:

> "At least nine climbers—two Nepalese, three Koreans, one each from Norway, Serbia, Ireland and Pakistan—were confirmed dead."

On August 3, 18:00 GMT, Deutsche Presse-Agentur reported:

> "A Swedish survivor feared in a radio interview that up to 11 climbers may have died.
>
> The accident was due to 'bad knowledge about the mountain, people that did not turn around in time and relied on others rather than their own skills,' the man named Strang told Swedish radio

news from a base camp at 5100m, after making his descent from some 8000m.

Officially, however, half a dozen climbers, including two Austrians, and one each from France and the Netherlands have been declared missing."

Amidst this wild news, EverestNews.com suggested:

"We are seeing a lot of confusing reports on the web and in the newspapers; we are sure people are trying to do their best. There is mass confusion. We understand some do not want the names of the dead released, but that does add to the confusion and mess. Let's start from the beginning..."

And, then, they bravely posted the "K2 dead list".

"Dead: 2 Pakistani Porters, Serb climber DREN MANDIC, and Norwegian Rolf Bae (his family wishes further information and details not be reported on him), two Nepalese, three Koreans, names of the three Nepalese and Koreans have not be released. Source of the Korean and Nepalese deaths include Ghulam Mohammed, owner of the Blue Sky Treks and Tour. (That would total nine.)"

Then, Mike Farris, the leader of American International team, called a special team meeting with his team members to count the dead. He updated his blog with: "Up to eleven climbers dead, or missing and presumed dead." Of course, EverestNews.com quoted this article to report on the status of the tragedy. They also updated details on two victims:

"Two of the dead climbers have come from the rescue efforts. Somewhat important to point out that these men were trying to save others, while the names are being [with]held. These men, while not American or European, have given their lives trying to save others and should be honored the same as if they were Western climbers.

After the ice broke lose on the bottleneck the Sherpa climber managed to descend to Camp 4 but he went back to help others. We are told he reached his friend but both slipped and died..."

And then, EverestNews.com released the general list of dead: [192]

> **The list of dead**:
> Day one (on the way UP): Serb climber DREN MANDIC and Pakistani climber name withheld; (2)
> Descent: Hwang Dong-Jin, Park Gyeong-Hyo and Kim Hyo-Gyeong all Korean (source Korean expedition); one Sherpa, name withheld; Rolf Bae (his family wishes further information and details not be reported on him) (5)
> Gerard McDonnell Irish still missing and the French leader HUGUES still missing . . . (2, "Missing".)
> Rescuers: One Sherpa and One Pakistani climber; names are being withheld at this time. (2)
> That is 11.

Eleven dead or missing presumed dead! Everyone was wondering how this could have happened on a perfect summit day. It was as yet a mystery.

---

[192] http://www.everestnews.com/pak2008/k22008sadnews080920080101.htm

Fifty-two

After finding Wilco, Norit and K2BC climbers made a last-ditch effort to bring him down to K2BC. Now, the focus of news shifted to the descent of Wilco and Marco. Marco was regarded as the last survivor.

Back at Camp 4, Marco got up late on Sunday morning and started his descent to Camp 3 alone on the Abruzzi. Singaporean team climbers had started heading down to K2BC. Since Marco, the last survivor, was descending and the Korean team had already done so, there was no reason for the Singapore team to stand by any longer. They also needed to look after their weakening bodies at the high camp. So, they were going down.

Roberto at K2BC has been in crisis management mode, too. He was desperate for Marco's descent, since the frostbitten Italian was not okay high up. Marco had to come down as soon as possible. Roberto even wanted to offer money if someone could go up to help Marco. He put pressure on the Italian Embassy to make rescue efforts.[193]

It was George Dijmarescu and his two Sherpas who volunteered to go up to help Marco down. George had come to K2 with his Romanian clients and had seen the disaster unfold. His decision to help somebody was a sacrifice. In the book *High Crime* by Michael Kodas, George was described as a bad character who had an undeserved reputation in Nepal. But here at K2 he was a Good Samaritan.

While George's team was about to continue its climb up from Camp 1, the Korean team was descending from above. Chuck of Tall American K2 & Broad Beak Expedition saw this as a danger factor because of the potential for stones to fall from above. He urged George's team to wait. Chuck's team had switched the challenge from Broad Peak to K2. Andy came to K2BC first, and now his teammates Dave and Chuck also joined K2BC.

At noon, a spokesperson from the Italian Embassy had announced:

---

[193] http://andyselters.wordpress.com/tag/k2/

"Pakistan army would send a helicopter to rescue Marco. There is a possibility Marco could come down today."

But here at K2, the scenario was different from the Alps. Epic stories of helicopter rescues in high Alpine mountains exist, but helicopter rescues at K2 were unheard of. In fact, the Pakistani military helicopter had a limitation in that it didn't have a winch to lower a cable and hoist the climber up. No helicopter would come to K2BC if the weather was unstable because of the risk of strong winds.

Marco barely arrived at Camp 3 on the Abruzzi route. After finding an energy bar and a drink in one of the abandoned tents, he decided to sleep there.

Wilco, Pemba and Cas on the Cesen route had descended the K2 slope, a day-long ordeal. By the time they finally reached the bottom of K2[194] Wilco had seriously frostbitten feet, which needed emergency treatment from Eric. When they checked in their mess tent, it was 9.30pm. Around that time, the Korean team had also returned to K2BC.

Wilco was confused for a while when he saw them. He wondered whether they were the Korean climbers he saw on the mountain. Wilco was in a lot of pain. While Chris and Chhiring were helping Eric to treat the two climbers, Wilco said at some point:

"And I think we slept still above 8000m."

Since his words were disjointed, they couldn't figure out what he had said. The treatment took the entire night. Pemba left the tent and eased himself quietly down into the kitchen tent.

Returning to their camp after finishing the treatments, Eric and Chhiring noticed that Pemba was sat deep in the kitchen tent having a hushed conversation with the Korean team Sherpas and passing a digital camera back and forth.[195]

---

[194] http://www.summitpost.org/wilco-and-cas-after-arriving-bc/565472
[195] p. 95, *One Mountain Thousand Summits* by Freddie Wilkinson

Fifty-three

August 4, D+3, Monday morning
K2BC was shrouded in a somber mist of death and injuries. Some climbers were spending their time going round to offer condolences at the various camps. In the morning, the Norit team received a message:

"Rescue helicopters are on the way to airlift the injured climbers!"

Wilco sat upright in the mess tent to direct Roeland in packing up their team's gear. But the wheels were about to fall off when a Korean came to the tent and accused Wilco:

"How come? How could you come down alone and abandon the climbers?"

Abandon the climbers? It was an embarrassing moment for Wilco. And people around him were also surprised. It was the first time they had heard the word "abandonment". The Korean climber was obviously at odds with Wilco over the climbers' deaths. But Wilco had plenty of reasons to throw the question back at the Korean. He had faced a similar situation of ethical questions while climbing the top of Everest in 2004 so he quickly retorted:

"I had to survive, as well."

It was a sensitive response to a gut-wrenching injury. But no one could understand its implication.

'What happened?'

'Does Wilco know something about the climbers' deaths?'

The tension eventually dissipated when the Korean walked away.

A team was needed to carry Wilco on a stretcher to the chopper site, and a group of people came to help. For lifting and carrying, Hoselito Bite and Andy Selters led the group. Wilco filmed K2BC with his camcorder from the red stretcher.[196]

---

[196] http://andyselters.wordpress.com/tag/k2/

Around 9am, the helicopter arrived and airlifted Wilco.[197] He would be flown to the closest medical unit, Skardu's Combined Military Hospital.

While the Serbian team members were trekking out from K2BC, Cecilia was hurriedly leaving K2BC. Bjorn Sekkesaeter, the media spokesperson for the Norwegian team, was coming from Norway to rescue her from the anticipated media frenzy. Her teammates quickly arranged a porter to go with her. Before her departure, she, Øystein and Lars allowed K2 Base Camp colleagues to take the last K2BC photograph. The American Andy also took a photograph.[198]

Around noontime, another helicopter arrived at K2BC for Cas. Before airlifting him, the helicopter picked up Roberto for an aerial search. When it surged into the air, people at K2BC saw the rare K2 airshow hovering around the mountain. The pilot spotted Marco descending Black Pyramid but he was over the flying limit of the helicopter. The pilot had to go down, and it flew away to Skardu after picking Cas up.

Government subsidiary Askari Aviation operated the helicopter service. The Dutch expedition was the 15th air rescue service they had undertaken in this Karakorum season. A little later, Mohammed Ilyas, spokesperson of the Askari Aviation, announced to the local journalists:

> "Two Dutch climbers with frostbite were rescued by helicopter from the mountain."

He added:

> "Their limbs might have to be amputated because of the severity of their frostbite."

In Islamabad, Shahzad Qaiser, the secretary of the Ministry of Tourism announced Marco's status through the Associated Press.

> "He (Marco) was spotted by the helicopters at seven–thousands metres (22,966 feet) and he will be rescued when he comes to six thousand metres (19,685 feet). So the search is on and I am very

---

[197] http://www.businessinsider.com.au/the-summit-2008-k2-tragedy-2013 -10#confortola-and-van-rooijen-were-airlifted-from-the-mountainside-by- pakistani-rescue-helicopters-46

[198] http://andyselters.wordpress.com/tag/k2/

hopeful that he will be able to descend to that height–rather to that depth–where he could be rescued."

Shahzad also added that:

> "Three Koreans, two Pakistanis, two Nepalese, a Frenchman, a Norwegian, a Serb, and an Irish national died."
> "It's been confirmed now that 11 people were killed in the accident. It's the worst one on any of our peaks."

Shahzad had counted the numbers during a crisis meeting with the travel agencies at 11.30am.

Finally, George's team reached Marco. While Marco was resting at Camp 2 drinking melted water, he made calls to Italy using George's satellite phone. He spoke his brother Luigi about his ordeal:

> "Up there it was hell. During the descent, beyond 8,000 meters, due to the altitude and the exhaustion I even fell asleep in the snow and when I woke up I could not figure out where I was."
> "My hands are fine, while my feet are black from frostbite. Anyway I can walk and I want to descend to the base camp."

He also talked with Agostino Da Polenza, the head of Ev-K2-CNR, an Italian-based, high-altitude scientific research mountaineering group:

> "Of course, of course, I'll keep going. Imagine if I gave up now."

Shahzad also announced that Pakistani authorities were in contact with two Italian climbers, one on his way to base camp[199] and another already there.

> "The Italian climber, Marco Confortola, descended to 20,340 feet but bad weather forced officials to abort an attempted helicopter rescue."
> "We do not have any missing mountain climbers."

---

[199] http://goalexploration.com/s/K2.html#28

Sher Khan, a retired colonel and the vice-president of the Alpine Club of Pakistan, and who was one of Pakistan's most experienced climbers, added to the reporters:

> "On K2, when they're missing they're dead... Anybody hit by an avalanche above the Bottleneck will be swept way down the South Face, and there's no way they'll ever find them."

It was a brutal recapping. But it was a candid reality.

Fifty-four

August 4, D+3, Monday afternoon
After the first treatment for his frostbitten toes, Wilco received a phone call from a journalist in Islamabad. Kamran Haider was a correspondent for news agency Reuters. Kamran interviewed Wilco and the story that ran was: K2 survivor recounts fatal mistakes, numbed panic.

Looking back and speaking by phone from his hospital bed, Wilco lamented the failure of the corporate agreement and pointed to the mistakes made in preparing for the final ascent as being partly responsible for the loss of life.

> "The biggest mistake we made was that we tried to make agreements."
> "Everybody had his own responsibility and then some people did not do what they promised."[200]

Until then, no one knew how the disaster occurred. Some light was finally starting to be shed on the disaster, but it sounded complicated. Was Wilco on course to win the blame game against other teams?

Wilco was recounting the K2 tragedy when another phone call came from Islamabad. His words of blame were passed around with dizzying speed. This time, he was interviewed by a Pakistani journalist, probably, Sadaqat Jan for the Associated Press. AP uploaded the story: Frostbitten Climbers Saved From K2 Avalanche. Stephen Graham, AP writer, updated and distributed it on 8/4/2008 4:58pm.

> "Everything was going well to Camp Four and on summit attempt everything went wrong... We were astonished, we had to move it.

---

[200] www.reuters.com/article/2008/08/04/us-pakistan-climbers-survivor-idUSISL3480720080804

That took, of course, many, many hours. Some turned back because they didn't trust it any more."

Cas joined Wilco in the same hospital room.[201] He had escaped serious injury to his hands. Geo News had come to the hospital, and filmed the footage, exclusively. Did the Pakistani Tourism agency play their part in the game by letting journalists conduct interviews with injured climbers who couldn't go anywhere?

In Europe and North America, the articles, images and footage were beginning to be spun by a variety of news agencies. USA TODAY had reported on the K2 tragedy: 11 feared dead after K2 avalanche; 3 men rescued. [202] Fox News reported: Three Climbers Rescued From K2; 11 Feared Dead.[203] CNN reported: K2 climbers rescued after avalanche claims 11.[204]

Meanwhile, the Korean Associated Press news agency reported the three Korean climbers' status as "Missing". On August 4, they upgraded the status into "Deaths":

> **K2; The deaths of three missing Korean climbers have been confirmed**[205]
> "On August 1, five Korean climbers summited on the top of K2, the second highest mountain, but unfortunately they lost three lives during their descent . . . They were Hwang Dong-Jin (45·Gyeong Nam Mountaineering Association), Kim Hyo-Gyeong (33·Ulsan Climbing Club) and Park Kyeong-Hyo (29 Gyeong Nam Mountaineering Association).[206]
> The foreign climbers took some photographs of the missing three climbers with their digital cameras, and showed them...

---

[201] https://www.youtube.com/watch?v=n2ch0-YvzgY

[202] http://usatoday30.usatoday.com/news/topstories/2008-08-03-520047825_x.htm

[203] http://www.foxnews.com/story/2008/08/04/three-climbers-rescued-from-k2-11-feared-dead/#ixzz2PkppO400

[204] http://www.nickrice.us/index_files/k2dispatch66.htm

[205] Reported by Dong-a Ilbo: 2008.08.04 13:52 / edited: 2008.08.04 14:28

[206] http://www.newsway.co.kr/view_sok.php?tp=1&ud=200808050943200040106&mod=1

Team leader Kim Jae-Su and woman climber Go Mi-Young (Kolon Sport) who summited together had escaped the disaster by making an earlier descent. They are searching the accident area."

As the world slowly learned the full extent of the disaster, the climbers' deaths triggered global criticism about unsafe climbing. Reinhold Messner told N24, the German television news channel that:

> "People today are booking these K2 package deals almost as if they were buying some all-inclusive trip to Bangkok,"
> "(Reaching the summit after dark) is just pure stupidity, that is not professional."[207]

Such criticism of the disaster wouldn't hold water; it prompted some people to accuse Reinhold of bias. They defended the climbers as top mountaineers, and justified their decisions and actions as the right ones. Among them, Tom of ExWeb—who had sold some climbing equipment like satellite phones to the Norit and Korean teams—defended the climbers:

> "So it's a little hard to say: 'That was the wrong decision, you should have a [cutoff] time.'
> "You really should have a cap of time. But sometimes things happen that make you change your decision . . . This accident can't be put on the climbers, that they've been careless."

American Chris Warner who summited K2 the previous year (2007) told the New York Times:

> "I think there were some tactical errors made, but it wasn't the tactics that killed them... You can point and say: 'They got to the summit at 8 o'clock [in the dark]'. That was a mistake, but it wasn't what killed them. You can say 'those people on oxygen probably ran out of oxygen...' But that's not what killed them. What killed them was the ice fall."

---

[207] http://www.spiegel.de/international/world/just-pure-stupidity-eleven-climbers-die-in-k2-disaster-a-569997.html

Ice fall? Had the cause of the disaster been steered in that direction when there were still many questions over the climbers' deaths and nobody actually knew the cause yet?

Fifty-five

Back at K2 Base Camp, it was all over! The Korean team that lost five teammates also sought a way to notify the victims' families. From day one of the disaster, the team got in touch with their mountaineering club in Korea. On the Nepal side, cook Ngawang had done the agonizing job. When Ngawang called Jumic's family, he learned that Jumic, now dead, had become a father.

"Loss of Father, but a newborn baby? What a sad!"

K2BC people could hear the punching of the names of the dead and date of death onto tin plates. Each team was to visit Gilkey Memorial to add these stamped plates and conduct a farewell ceremony.

Meanwhile, Wilco and Cas were carried out from the hospital, and transported to a local hotel. Wilco was in a wheelchair.[208]

Wilco, sitting on the bed, was interviewed by journalists who entered his hotel room:

"I'm Wilco Van Rooijen from the Netherlands," he identified himself.[209]

And then, he started to talk about his ordeal and the chilling moments in K2.

"I came upon three Korean climbers," he said. "One sat dazed in the snow. Another held a rope. The third was suspended at the other end, hanging upside down. They were trying to survive, but I had also to survive because I was getting snow blind. I offered help but they declined, believing help was already on the way... They were thinking of using my gas, my rope!"

On his bed, Cas was listening quietly to Wilco's testimony.

---

[208] http://www.deseretnews.com/article/700248375/11-people-feared-dead-on-K2-crews-save-2-Dutch-1-Italian.html?pg=all

[209] https://www.youtube.com/watch?v=n2ch0-YvzgY

Wilco hadn't mentioned anything about the distressed Korean team climbers the previous day. Associated Press updated and shared this significant testimony. And the various world news media reported it: Dutch survivor of K2 avalanche recalls his ordeal.

Finally, Maarten of Norit NLBC announced Gerard and Hugues' deaths, officially:

> **Last Emergency Update** (4 August), K2BaseCamp–NL (23.30hr. K2–time 04/08/08)
> IMPORTANT MESSAGE:
> "We are very sorry to inform you that our friend and climbing partner Gerard McDonnell died while descending from K2 Summit. We deeply sympathize with Gerard's family in Ireland and his girlfriend Ann. Our friend Gerard will not return from K2. In addition we are also sad to inform you that Hugues d'Aubarede[210] died while descending from K2 Summit as already mentioned by other sources. We feel sorry for Hugues' family."

---

[210] http://pakistank2.blogspot.co.nz/

Fifty-six

August 5, D+4, Tuesday
The morale of K2BC was at rock bottom, its darkest days having continued as eleven climbers were confirmed killed. There were strong winds during the night. Tents were twisted. A light rain was falling from the early morning. It was certain the last survivor Marco would safely get down to K2BC that day.

The exodus from the infamous K2 had started. While packing up, teams had asked their travel agencies for porters for transport. But it was another battle for them to secure enough porters. It would take time. They were all sick of waiting. When would the porters come? Those were normal K2 hassles.

At 11.30am, the secretary of the Ministry of Tourism called K2BC. Captain Azeem, the liaison officer of the Korean team, confirmed the dead by calling out their names. And then, the secretary announced the official death toll:

1. Mr Kim Hyo-Gyeong / Korean
2. Mr Park Kyeong-Hyo / Korean
3. Mr Hwang Dong-Jin / Korean
4. Mr Jumic Bhote / Nepali
5. Mr Pasang Bhote / Nepali
6. Mr Jehan Baig / Pakistani HP
7. Mr Meherban Karim / Pakistani HP
8. Mr D'aubarede Hugues Jean-Louis Marie / French
9. Mr Gerard McDonnell / Irish
10. Mr Dren Mandic / Serbian
11. Mr Rolf Bae / Norwegian

The secretary gave his condolences to the Government of Pakistan and the national embassies concerned in Pakistan.

Eleven climbers died over the weekend. It was not only a devastating blow but also the deadliest two days in K2 history.

During the afternoon, some Korean team members visited Gilkey Memorial but Kim wasn't among them. He was busy with something else. Go, Shon, Lee and two Sherpas attached tin plate after tin plate. They also paid their last respects to Sherpa Jumic and Big Pasang, tying the plates with wires onto piles of stones. Tsering and Little Pasang were distraught at the deaths. They then had a brief ceremony for the dead with Soju, Korean wine and dried fish. The rain added their grief.

During that time, Kim had been struggling to cope with the deaths and apply logic to them.

'How can I justify these deaths?' Kim wondered.

Some K2BC climbers approached the team to console them over the deaths. The team had been torn apart by heartbreak over the disaster. Fred worked hard to generate more news and with his documentary film. He offered the team his condolences. When he asked Go and Kim for a statement on the accidents they felt frustrated speaking in English. So Fred, while filming, encouraged Kim to just go ahead and speak in Korean. Kim felt pressured by him. This kind of digging stirred up anger while the deaths crushed him. Since he knew something about Fred's engagement in Jehan's death at the Bottleneck base, Kim gave his general opinion on the climbers' deaths in the Himalayas. The American Andy noticed he talked about it for over half an hour.

The mood of the Korean team's camp remained somber. There was tension among the members and Sherpas over the deaths. It was not normal stress.

They needed liquid and drank in silence for hours, neither wanting to look at each other. Kim and Go waited for their helicopter, desperate for it to arrive. They arranged to catch it near BPBC but realized they would have to go on waiting. The next air service was for the Italian team. The desperate Kim also realized that other vultures were already circling Korean team climbers. To beat the poachers, 'Let them just wait until the porters come' turned out to be another disaster for him. The best he could do was to escape from here.

"My team became an incredibly shrinking team," he said.

"We need to get out of here, whatever!" Go replied.

"Let's call one more helicopter!"

The cost of two helicopters for all team members was incredibly expensive. But no payment, no helicopter. Money was no object in that desperate situation.

"We're going to abandon all heavy equipment like tents, mats and cooking utensils..." decided Kim.

Marco had reached Camp 1 with the help of George and Sherpas in the worsening weather conditions. He then continued down to ABC. K2BC climbers including his teammate Roberto went to ABC to receive him.

Finally, Marco arrived.[211] While he was resting there, more news on what Marco was doing and saying filtered out.

Late afternoon, Marco came down to K2BC.[212] As soon as he reached Chorten and saw the piles of stones, he fell face-down on the ground. He was the last survivor amid the 11 dead and was distraught about it. His toes were frostbitten. While Eric treated his injuries in Norit's mess tent, Marco tried to talk about something that had happened up the mountain. But it was hard for the others to understand.

In Ireland, Pat Falvey, who volunteered to be Gerard's family spokesman, made a comment on Gerard's death:

> "I'm afraid Gerard's been killed. We've heard from bc that Marco says he saw Gerard's yellow boots in the avalanche."

At Skardu, it was a waiting day in the hotel for Wilco and Cas.[213] The weather was no good for the flight.

---

[211] http://www.k2tallmountain.com/blog/K2_Tall_Mountain/Photos.html

[212] http://www.reuters.com/article/2008/08/05/us-pakistan-climbers-idUSISL3024620080805

[213] http://www.independent.co.uk/news/world/asia/death-or-glory-the-truth-about-k2-909516.html?action=gallery&ino=5

Fifty-seven

August 6, D+5, Wednesday morning

Because of the wine, some climbers managed to sleep without being haunted by nightmares for yet another night. The Korean camp didn't chase Marco. Instead, they were very busy packing from early morning. They piled all the large bags with gear and personal belongings outside the mess tent, ready to leave everybody by abandoning their tents.

Marco got a message that a helicopter was coming from Askari Aviation.

The Korean team also received this message; it was time to go. It was a great escape.[214] The heli-landing place was near Broad Peak Base Camp, two hours' walk away. Their four Pakistani staff also helped them to carry the heavy bags.

Around 9.30am, a helicopter came and landed in K2BC. It was for Marco and Roberto. After collecting them swiftly, the helicopter surged up in the air. People who saw the helicopter flying over their heads waved their hands saying:

"So long, Marco!"

Before leaving K2BC, Marco handed over a handsome amount of cash to Jelle for Pemba. Why not for George's team, who helped him down from Camp 2 to ABC? Was it a special gift or a bribe to Pemba for something? What's that about?

The Korean team had arrived at a flat landing zone site near Broad Peak Base Camp. They had to wait a few hours before for the helicopters to arrive. Surrounded by piles of bags at the rugged, stoney place, they all sat down with their backs to K2 where the victims' bodies remained.

It was an eerily quiet atmosphere. In the center, Tsering, Little Pasang and Nagwang sat together in loose formation. Tsering, downcast, was back

---

[214] http://www.mfarris.net/blog/page/5/

to back with Little Pasang, each holding the other up. Little Pasang seemed in a reflective mood about what had happened up on the mountain. His face showed how gut-wrenched he was feeling:

'What a ridiculous result! We were so close. There were several things we'd do differently. We could have rescued them if we had more manpower...'

Kim and No. 2 Kim were sitting together on the stones. They were smoking. Go had also lost her trademark smile. She bit her lip and tried to be strong, although her shine had turned into gloom. When Go received an SMS message out of nowhere, she showed it to Kim who was staring out into the distance.

The endless wait for the helicopters became boring. It was a fine day. Again, K2 looked stunning. Her revealing beauty was tempting for everyone. Finally, the Korean junior climbers found something to do. They started to pose for their last photographs with K2 in the background. They couldn't stare up at the mountain where colleagues were resting. Someone posed, his face showing his deep sympathy for the lost colleagues.

Lee, the oldest and ex-lawyer, sat apart from the group, staring off into the crevasses. The loss remained hard for him to swallow.

"This shouldn't happen," he said, to no one in particular.

For him, the fact of them being gone just seemed so unreal. Captain Azeem, the Korean team's liaison officer, went over to a flat site to mark the helipad.

Around that time, the remaining Norit team members were passing the Korean team. They had left K2BC[215] and were trekking to Skardu.

It was around 11.20am. Suddenly, they could hear the chopper's whirling blades.

"Taxi's here!" shouted the porters.

As usual, Captain Azeem went over to the helipad site to guide the helicopter down. Once it had landed on the marked place, the Korean team members rushed to load their bags, and then hopped into it. [216] This process took almost an hour.

As soon as the helicopter surged into the skies of Broad Peak, they heard another helicopter fly into the area and land in the same place. The porters and the rest of the Korean team members, including the liaison

---

[215] http://andyselters.wordpress.com/tag/k2/
[216] http://blog.daum.net/_blog/BlogTypeView.do?blogid=0Xolp&articleno
=37&categoryId=2®dt=20110202153932

officer, hurriedly loaded the remaining bags and then hopped into the helicopter. This second helicopter surged up into Broad Peak, and headed in the direction of Skardu.

That day, people around the area could hear many choppers. Kim Man-Su, a Korean trekker, also heard the sounds at Concordia. When he saw one of the choppers flying in midair, he quickly grabbed his camera and took a photograph, which is this book's cover.[217]

Man-Su had a resting day with his friends at Concordia. He had trekked to K2BC the previous day with his guide. There, he visited the Korean camp and met some members including Go. His hobby was taking photographs. [218] But then he didn't click his camera. The mood was too sad.

At K2BC, George had approached Pemba and asked him to speak out to ensure future understanding and clarification on the disaster. Instead, Pemba promised him:

"We will be sitting together in Kathmandu for further discussion on what I will have to say publicly about the disaster."

Meanwhile, when Eric who treated the survivors interviewed with NPR by saterlite call,[219] Marco and Roberto had suddenly landed at Paiyu—a half an hour away from Skardu, where they were supposed to be transferred to a military hospital as soon as possible.

The remaining issue was, who will pay the money for the helicopter rides? Pakistani people? The Italian Embassy (Italian people)? Or Marco?

Now, Maj. Farooq Feroz, Pakistan Army Spokesman, announced:

> "Today, Pakistani military army successfully rescued 13 Korean members and 2 Italian members."

The helicopters suddenly landed and unloaded the Korean team clients in the middle of nowhere. When they stepped out of the helicopters, they found themselves on a military runway where they would have to wait a further hour for a bigger chopper. Skardu by air was another hour away.

"It's so hot," exclaimed Shon.

"The heat waves are killing me," agreed Lee.

---

[217] http://www.indica.or.kr/xe/explore/2424737

[218] http://www.indica.or.kr/xe/explore/2424705

[219] http://www.npr.org/templates/story/story.php?storyId=93351112

They changed out of their climbing clothes and into the light t-shirts at the nearby restroom. While waiting, they had to find a refuge from the heat of the day under a big chopper beside the strip.

After the long wait, they hopped into the bigger chopper. It was around 3pm.

Once airborne, Shon took several in-flight pictures. The Korean team climbers stared at one another in silence, worrying about the future. Kim looked nervous. What was on his mind? Exhausted and tired, he felt naked here. His eyes were hidden behind dark sunglasses, but his nervous face was saying something. He was deep on thought about finding a way out.

Marco and Roberto had arrived at Skardu. They were immediately transported to the Skardu Hospital by a military landrover. [220] Italian Embassy and travel agency staff received them. Marco was transported from the car into the hospital by wheelchair. Many journalists who descended on the hospital were waiting for him. [221]

When his bandaged feet were unwrapped, it looked very serious, shading from magenta to black. His eyes were fixed on them for a long time, deeply worried. [222] When he put his feet on a pillow, a Pakistani doctor came and helped him to take off his upper clothes. After treatment, his feet were bandaged again. Journalists including photographer Muhammad Abbas were busy taking shots. The race was on for a scoop, with editors in the world's newsrooms able to score their own goal with the footage and raw articles coming from the hospital.

---

[220] http://zpravy.aktualne.cz/marco-confortola/r~i:photo:209421/r~i:article:612799/

[221] http://www.independent.co.uk/news/world/asia/death-or-glory-the-truth-about-k2-909516.html?action=gallery&ino=4

[222] http://cronacaeattualita.blogosfere.it/post/129499/tragedia-k2-confortola-mi-amputeranno-tutte-e-dieci-le-dita-dei-piedi

Fifty-eight

Wilco was meantime being interviewed over the phone by Kirkpatrick Reardon, the journalist of National Geographic Adventure (NGA). It was too early to speculate on the exact cause of the accident. It could take months or years to find sufficient evidence and uncover the truth. When Kirkpatrick asked a hard question about what caused the avalanche, Wilco answered:

> "It wasn't a real avalanche. An avalanche is a lot of snow. It was a serac that fell down and that was the only explanation for killing three people."[223]

Had the Bottleneck serac really collapsed? Probably, this was Wilco's personal opinion.

When NGA posted this interview on its blog, reader's responses popped up, and some readers cast strong doubts on Wilco's claim about the serac killing climbers.

> "The avalanche / serac fall happened BELOW him. In the DARK. How COULD he see it? It is way out of bounds for any of us to second guess the recall of a survivor, especially in such extreme situations.
> It's actually amazing that he has the presence of so MUCH recall; most of us would have been effectively brain dead—and therefore completely dead."[224]

> "And he didn't see the avalanche, but it took the rope away! Strange indeed. A lot of questions need to be answered!!!!"[225]

---

[223] http://adventureblog.nationalgeographic.com/2008/08/06/k2-survivor-wilco-van-rooijen/
[224] Posted by: Brian Boerman | August 14, 2008 at 03:12pm

Wilco has never answered these comments.

It was late afternoon when Marco got treatment in his hospital bed. Journalists then started to ask questions and Marco recounted his ordeal. [226] Muhammad Abbas of Associated Press reported: Tragic Toll After Chaos on Mountain. The Italian news agency ANSA reported Marco words:

> "A 656–foot rope, very light but strong... was not brought by a somewhat sloppy porter, which was just the beginning of the problems.
> "When the second avalanche was occurred, Gerard disappeared and Pemba saved me.
> "I think we arrived late on the summit of K2 because the technical equipment was low quality."

Sloppy porter? On that day, Scott Peterson the staff writer of The Christian Science Monitor wrote an article: In K2 aftermath, lessons learned. New York Times wrote an article: What Happened on K2's Summit.

---

[225] Posted by: lorrsi | August 14, 2008 at 01:01pm
[226] http://argomenti.ilsole24ore.com/marco-confortola.html

Fifty-nine

August 7, D+6, Thursday

In the early morning, Wilco and Cas were transported to Skardu airport and then took a Pakistani Airways flight, arriving at 8am at Islamabad Airport.

They were transported to the Regency Hotel at Rawalpindi by van, which was arranged by their travel agency. When they arrived at the hotel reception, a dozen reporters from various sources were waiting them. Wilco and Cas instinctively knew they were newsmakers so they agreed to a big interview session in the hotel lobby.

Sitting on a long sofa and putting his thickly bandaged frostbitten feet on the lower table, Wilco relaxed and said:

> "My experience in K2 was wonderful experience because we were successful on reaching the summit after three times and thirteen years. But on the other hand of course it's disaster that you are losing a team members."[227]

Cas added:

> "When you were working together on the mountain; working very hard to reach summit. When you reaching summit, so very successful, then after one day descending they discover that one team member is gone, it's not nice."

It was a goldmine for photographers Tanveer Shahzad, Emillio Morenatti, Farooq Naeem and others.[228] They took many shots of Wilco and Cas.

---

[227] www.youtube.com/watch?v=Sy4g6w_BvfE

[228] http://rue89.nouvelobs.com/2008/08/18/k2-comment-la-montagne-tueuse-a-englouti-onze-hommes

Marco had changed clothes into a light blue t-shirt with sponsor logos on the front. They were then transported to the Italian Embassy, Marco being wheeled there in a wheelchair.

A dozen reporters and photographers were already milling around in the ambassador's room. Sitting on the sofa, Marco started to explain his K2 ordeal to Ambassador Vincentzo Prati and the surrounding journalists.

> "We were all prepared. All alpine climbers. We were people who knew what we were doing, but it was K2, the most difficult of mountains.
>
> "In the morning, we set out again and after a short while, we came across three climbers from South Korea, hanging upside down, held by a cord attached to their waists. Two were unconscious. For three hours, McDonnell and I tried to right them, but it was in vain.
>
> "All three died. It was at that moment, "for some strange reason", that McDonnell began to walk away. It was the last time I would see my friend alive. Exhausted, I fell asleep, only to be woken by an ominous rumbling.
>
> "All of a sudden I saw an avalanche coming down. It was only 20 metres to my right. I saw the body of Gerard sweep past me."

Marco was a tough guy, but he couldn't stop crying when he talked about Gerard's death. The ambassador was captivated by Marco's story and shook his head as if it was hard to believe what Marco was saying.

Later, Omar Waraich's report headlined: "I was desperate, hopeless, but I wasn't going to give up," says K2 survivor.

Reuters also reported it, and later released video footage.

Since the major teams were converging on Islamabad, something was looming. The Ministry of Tourism had announced there would be an official press conference soon.

However, where was the grief-stricken Korean team who had lost five climbers—nearly half of the victims? [230] They were near Skardu, arriving in the afternoon. With all media eyes on Marco and Wilco, they'd been overlooked. Their escape from K2BC in the cold had turned into heat. Hot and tired, they sat in their travel agent's office and drank chilled coke.

---

[230] http://www.8264.net/html/fair-events/other-events/200808/14-2013.html

Sixty

August 8, D+7, Friday

Friday was the rest day in Pakistan. A week after he had stood on the summit of the world's deadliest peak, Wilco unwrapped his bloody bandages from his frostbitten feet. He was surprised. The toes were hideously swollen. He needed immediate treatment.

A western specialist was arranged. A staff member from his travel agency came to help them. Wilco, Cas and the staff went down to the hotel lobby so they could wait for the Spanish doctor team. Wilco put his foot on the table, while Cas checked online news from the team's laptop. When Cas was checking some images, he wasn't sure of their meaning.

However, they moved to Wilco's room to treat his feet. Then, Marco and Roberto came to the hotel. They wanted to see Wilco but this wasn't possible while Wilco's feet were being treated.[231] Why were the Italians there? Was there some serious business left for Marco? Or was Marco simply seeking his summit images from Cas's camera?

When Cas met Marco and Roberto in the hotel lobby, journalists swamped them again. ExWeb's Pakistani correspondent Karrar Haidri joined in. Everyone wanted to understand the disaster. When journalists asked Marco questions about the unfolding events, Marco boldly explained it in detail. Cas and Roberto sitting next to Marco could listen the story vividly from him. To be clear, Marco often drew sketches on paper.[232]

"Gotta run!" said Marco suddenly, after taking a call.

Marco and Roberto withdrew themselves from the hotel. Why?

---

[231] http://www.everestnews.com/pak2008/k22008sadnewsfund080820080
1012008.htm

[232] http://himalman.wordpress.com/2008/08/18/himalaya-2008-climbing-
season-karakoram-and-himalaya-wrap-up-8-week-in-review/

It was unusual for the government offices of the Ministry of Tourism to open on the rest day. They had to handle the emergency before their chances disappeared.

The Ministry finally stepped in to undertake a thorough investigation. It had announced a press conference and, beforehand, invited all the climbers into its meeting room. One message was clear; that they would not allow the climbers 'out of Pakistan' without this procedure. In hindsight, the Ministry was going to tap the teams' minds on the disaster so they could look into what had gone wrong.

Meanwhile, a blame war has been looming since there was some bitterness between the teams over the deaths. They were once friends, but had always been different guys with different styles and had never been close. It was so easy to become enemies, but they'd just been doing their job. The Korean team had serious business with Wilco and Marco. Some had reacted angrily to their one-sided news about the dead. Wilco might want to know how the Koreans could get on a fast track for Islamabad?

But Marco and Roberto avoided the meeting. The facts around their debrief are unknown. Diplomatic lines were at work. Maybe, these high-level talks bought them an exemption. What a privilege! But it was unfair as far as finding out the truth was concerned.

The Himalayas were unique and the Pakistani side showed it on that day.

At 2.30pm, the Norit and Korean team members turned up in the Green Trust Tower—the government building. They were going to have a showdown meeting at a conference room of the Ministry of Tourism in the twelfth floor of the building.

All 13 Korean team members came in. They had their say. Wilco and Cas were there with their liaison officer and a travel agent. Wilco had changed his clothes into his favorite orange jacket, which had become his trademark since K2BC.

A group of Pakistani officials and Pakistani climbing leaders were waiting for them at the conference room. They sat around a long, large conference table. The Ministry didn't allow any journalists to listen in on the meeting.

Shahzad Qaiser, the secretary of Pakistan's Ministry of Tourism, headed the meeting. He sat at the edge of the long table. To his right was Ashraf Aman, who was the first Pakistani summiteer of K2 in 1977. He was running a travel and tourism-based company ATP. To his left was Nazir Sabir—president of the Alpine Club of Pakistan. Besides a 1981 K2, he became the first man from Pakistan to climb Everest in 2000. He was also the boss of the travel agency that had supported the Serbian expedition.

The climbers took their seats around the table. On the secretary's right, Kim, Go, Mrs Song, Captain Azeem, Lee (S-R), Lee (W-S) and Little Pasang took their seats side by side. Behind the row, sat a group of officials from the Ministry of Tourism. The only odd slot in the lineup was Brigadier M. Bashir Baz, the head of Askari Aviation, but his presence made sense.

On the secretary's left were the Norit team's travel agent, Wilco, Cas, Kiani the Norit team's liaison officer, Tsering, Kim (T-G) and Shon, all seated in row. Opposite the secretary was No. 2 Kim and so on.

The secretary handled most of the talking. When the brigadier was speaking about the Pakistani mountain and air service, the secretary glared at everyone sitting around since the climbers exchanged mixed responses. Tempers were flaring over the long table.

Wilco was sitting quietly, crossing his legs. His counterpart Kim didn't see him. His eyes were downcast, checking his handset, but Go sat remaining remarkably straight-faced. The oldest Lee and the oldest woman Song were staring at the secretary. The team's liaison officer was in charge of videotaping the meeting. Tsering's eyes were down, checking the images in his digital still camera, while Shon kept taking pictures.

When the possible cause of Jehan's death was mentioned, the blame game went on and on. More critics were making some people defenders. Wilco was already speaking of the problem of the Haps. He tried to talk about this point further.

"Sucks . . . !" said Kim.

And then Kim turned on Wilco:

"Shut up and back off! They were killed because of you!"

Wilco felt thoroughly ambushed. They had had many meetings at K2BC and knew the reasons all too well. Was there a war of words? If yes, how could it be possible? Was Kim's knee-jerk reaction a calculated strike? Did Wilco and Cas feel Kim's rebukes inwardly? Was Kim successful in neutralizing this force?

Everyone in the room was stunned. The peaceful talks quickly turned ugly. No one knew what to do.

"I've never seen this before," remarked Qaiser.

The slurs and the standoff had already ruined the meeting. Nazir Sabir stood up saying:

"That's enough!"

And then he marched from the room. But Kim chased him. Why? Did he know that Nazir's great scheme had gone badly? There was another round of bizarre confrontation, with fiery clashes between the teams over the deaths. The meeting ended in a walkout.

The Ministry might have wanted to find out something important through holding the meeting. But their attempt failed miserably. Everyone was shattered. The climbers got all-clear. They were free to go. They could go home!

The mood changed when the Korean team stepped out the building. Korean Embassy officials were waiting for them. Kim and Go had big smiles on their faces.

Sixty-one

August 9, D+8, Saturday
Wilco's feet were not okay. That was another sign of things getting serious. He was eager to get the hell out of Pakistan and go home. But there was a reason he had to stay. Gerard's family was coming from Ireland to see him. The family has endured days and nights of false hopes. The family's pain deserved answers.

In Ireland, the media has been in full cry with Gerard's K2 summit news.

> Irish adventurer tops the world[233]
> Limerick native becomes first Irishman to scale K2[234]

However, on Sunday August 3, Gerard's family and friends were shocked and devastated to learn of the tragedy. Irish President Mary McAleese sent a condolence message to the family:

> "Following so closely on their righteous pride, and that of the country, at Gerard becoming the first Irish person to scale K2, it is truly heartbreaking that they must now contemplate the loss of a beloved son and brother."

The family was ripped apart by the death. While their thoughts were on the memorial service, Gerard's brother-in-law Damien issued a family statement for Gerard's family:

> "We are extremely proud of the many heroic and brave achievements of Gerard, whose death has left a major void in our

---

[233] August 2, http://www.herald.ie
[234] August 2, Belfasttelegraph.co.uk

lives. He brought honour not only to us, his family, but the whole country when he became the first Irishman to summit K2."

Gerard's mentor Pat Falvey also wrote an article that appeared in the Irish *Independent* on Monday, August 4: Ger died doing what he loved: touching the void. And the media reported the news:

Body of Limerick man will not be recovered from K2
Family mourns loss of K2 climber[235]
Ireland Mourns Its Latest Hero[236]

Andrew Buncombe wrote an article: Since Nine die in worst-ever K2 climbing disaster, on the Independent.co.uk:

"Even now, all the details of the disaster are unclear. But, pieced together from interviews with survivors and other first-hand accounts, what follows is an attempt to explain what happened when things went drastically wrong on the Savage Mountain."

On August 5, Jerome Taylor posted an article: The Big Question: What makes K2 the most perilous challenge a mountaineer can face?, writing at length on the Independent.co.uk.

Meanwhile, on August 3–4, Gerard's partner Annie was coming from Alaska to Ireland to join Gerard's family. Family friends had arranged the travel to Pakistan for Annie, his brother JJ and his girlfriend Ceren and sister Denise with her husband Damien. They're going to meet Wilco and Norit team members at Islamabad. Media reported about it.

Family of K2 climber to fly to Pakistan (August 4)
Family seek explanations for what went wrong (Colm Kelpie and Jason O'Brien, August 5)
Last survivor hears of tragedy after arrival at K2 base camp (Jason O'Brien, August 6)

---

[235] http://www.independent.ie/irish-news/family-mourns-loss-of-k2-climber-26500457.html
[236] http://thelede.blogs.nytimes.com/ August 4, 2008, 10:22am

On August 9, Omar Waraich the independent journalist reported in Islamabad: "I was desperate, hopeless, but I wasn't going to give up," says K2 survivor.

The Italians were in the Islamabad airport waiting to go home. Marco had shaved his head, probably in honor of the dead.

In the afternoon, the Korean team with its liaison officer turned up to the office of the Alpine Club of Pakistan in Islamabad. The Club was the one that issues government permits. It was conducting debrief and then issuing the summit certificate. In particular, the helicopter rescues were user-pays and recorded as such in the record book. The climbers needed to claim any refundable money from their deposits.

How much the Korean team paid for their helicopter rides is unknown. The secretary of the Club eventually handed over summit certificates to Kim and Go, and then shook hands with each person. Kim blankly looked at it and thought:

'Is this paper all I get in exchange for five lives?'

Vanity! Karrar, the ExWeb correspondent, asked Kim and Go many questions about the climb and the disaster when they sat back to the table. Go gave him a postcard with her cute signature on it.

To 클라르
Be happy. MiSun Go[237]

Finally, Gerard's family landed in Islamabad. At first, the family met the Italian consulate, instead of Marco.

---

[237] http://www.explorersweb.com/everest_k2/news.php?id=17484

Sixty-two

August 10, D+9, Sunday

Marco and Roberto arrived at Milan Airport in the morning. The pair met the press at the airport. Security personnel wheeled Marco to the conference room where more journalists were eagerly awaiting them.

When a reporter asked that "What happened on K2?" Marco explained:

> "The story of the rescue is that I tried three or four hours to give help to those guys. It's something that just came from my heart. It was after that I paid the consequences."

Marco had a small scar on the back of his head. It must have occurred when something hit him during his descent at the Bottleneck or Camp 2.[238] Marco also told Italian news channel Sky TG24:

> "To try to help, to save the others, I froze my feet and hands... But instinct makes you want to save them, and for me that's a good thing."

The grieving family was going to meet with Wilco and Cas during the afternoon. Since Wilco's terrible debacle the previous day, he had feared the family's condemnation of Gerard's death. Cas prepared five sheets of canvas-sized maps and drawings.

When Wilco and Cas arrived at the appointed house, Wilco was nervous. Annie opened the door. After an emotional meeting with the family, the conversation started. Everyone wanted to understand what happened over Gerard's death. The meeting took place over several hours. Cas showed the maps and drawings, and explained what probably happened.

---

[238] www.youtube.com/watch?v=p5JFSonb8dE

"There were two avalanches—first, on the bottom section of the Traverse and second, on the Bottleneck," he said, pointing to those locations.

Two avalanches? But, it was an explanation only, with no evidence. As the conversation waned, so questions on the exact circumstances of Gerard's death were confused. The family realized that Wilco was scratching his head about it. The vague explanation led to unnecessary assumptions. The family had to talk with Pemba, who was hiking out from K2BC.

On that day, Maarten of NLBC posted on his team's blog a short comment. First, he praised Pemba's rescue effort as heroic! And second, he wrote about the status of the rest of the Norit members (Team 2) including Pemba. They had been trekking down from K2BC and arrived at Skardu that evening.

August 11, D+10, Monday

Belfasttelegraph.co.uk posted an article: K2 survivor (Marco) tells of his final moments with Irish hero Gerard McDonnell—'He comforted dying climbers for three hours'.

On one of those days, Wilco met Matthew Power of *Mens Journal* and stressed the following points in the interview:

> "I have nothing to hide... With this tragedy, if you're really surprised about this, then you don't understand anything about it. If you don't want to face the risk, don't go to K2."[239]

Nothing to hide? Then, the remaining Norit team members (Pemba, Mark, Jelle and Roeland) finally arrived at Skardu after a six-day journey.

ExWeb issued a ten-page report: ExplorersWeb Week in Review Special K2 Edition. It also reported Gerard's death quoting Marco's testimony as below:

> "I saw my friend Gerard's boots falling among the blocks of ice and snow."

However, ExWeb left room about the causes of the deaths:

---

[239] http://www.mensjournal.com/magazine/k2-the-killing-peak-2012 0503?page=9

"Details were not yet known about how or if Gerard, Hugues and Rolf had died."

August 12, D+11, Tuesday

The flight between Skardu and Islamabad was notoriously unreliable. It was often canceled because of poor weather. At 5am, the remaining Norit members started to hit the road from Skardu, and they arrived in Islamabad late in the evening.

Meanwhile, where was Cecilia? Didn't Bjorn, the media spokesperson for the Norwegian team, urgently come to Pakistan from Norway so he could protect her from the media frenzy?

The Korean team, around 2pm, was at Islamabad International airport to get a plane bound for Bangkok.

When they arrived in Bangkok after a few hours' flight, they waited a few more hours in the airport's transit room before boarding a night flight to Korea. They looked relaxed, smiling. However, it was the calm before the storm. They were about to face blame from all sides. It would be their darkest hours. On board, these thoughts began to sink in. They looked wretched and sad. The in-flight pictures taken by Shon are evidence of that. They feared the coming events.

"You'll be all right, " said one of the senior members.

The juniors Shon (B-W), Lee (S-R) and Kim (T-G) were driven to follow suit. The team had planned their responses, devised strategies and called their club people in Korea.

Sixty-three

August 13, D+12, Wednesday
Amid global news coverage of the K2 disaster, Kim and his team members arrived at Incheon International airport in Korea. Journalists eagerly awaited them, despite the early hour of the morning. They asked questions, but Kim walked past them without making any comment. Someone had also directed the climbers not to speak to the press. They shied away from the media and were effectively herded onto a hired tour bus without a press conference. The bus drove away somewhere.

From the outset of the K2 disaster, the team's mountaineering club was in a state of emergency. They got the disastrous news on day one (D+1) from the mountain direct. Cho Hyung-Kyu, who was the president of the mountaineering club 'kafgyeongnam', had acted swiftly to tell the media. He released a press statement which said nothing about the events. It was day two (D+2), Monday afternoon. Since then, not only the club but also the Korean Alpine Federation had called emergency sessions over the deaths.

The public eye had shifted to the well-informed media reports on the heated gold medal news from the 2008 Beijing Olympic Games. News on the K2 disaster was treated as local news.

As usual, the government authority had not treated the climbers' deaths as suspicious. Only the club kafgyeongnam had struggled with the press. The club's top priority has been stabilizing the disaster. *First,* it was planned that Kim would front up to the victims' families and journalists, and *second,* a funeral was planned to be held. That was the procedure to wrap up the disaster, and it was important for the families' and public closure. For it, the club had backed Kim since day two.

During the afternoon of August 13, the tour bus arrived at Kum Kang Hospital in Gim Hae where the funeral was to be held. When Kim and team members stepped out from the bus, they were greeted by Cho and several club members. Some presses were present, so they might get themselves on television. With Cho's guide, Kim and his team members formed a block to enter the funeral parlor's corridor where many flower-decorated wreaths were paraded with clubs' flags. Requiem music was playing through the speakers.

As soon as they entered the room where three enlarged photo-frames symbolizing the dead were placed, they bowed down with their faces to the floor. After putting flowers onto the table, they moved to the room where the families had been waiting for them. Seeing the victims' families was another heartbreaking moment.

"Where is my son? You went together. But why have you only returned?" they asked.

The families wept aloud and expressed their feelings of loss for husbands or sons. They never expected that they would not return from K2. Until now, the families had endured the mystery surrounding the deaths.

It was time for the climbers and the families to front up to the media in a big room.

Behind Kim, stood the No. 2 man Kim Seong-Sang, Shon Byung-Woo, Lee Seung-Rok and Kim Tae-Gyu. Ms Go was not there. Someone had successfully managed to divert her away at Incheon airport.

Kim wore blue jeans and a checked shirt. His blue cap had the Kolon brand on it. Was he looking for advertising impact? It's a commercial world. The media cameras, including *MBC TV*, were rolling.

Kim was in showdown. He started with an apology to the families.

"I bow my head in apology to the family of the victims," he said.

He lowered his eyes to the ground, but told about the final moments of the accident.

"At 8211m of the Bottleneck, a serac of 100m in height had collapsed. And the avalanche swept away the fixed rope, then accidents happened... We rushed to send the rescue team, but they died in the collapse of the serac... While the climbers were climbing down the last section of the Bottleneck, the serac had collapsed and the victims were swept away by it. On the top of that, the avalanche swept away the two Sherpas."

Kim was efficient with words. He did not use half-measures, delivering his statement with convincing authority. However, 'Bottleneck? Serac? Died by the serac at the Bottleneck . . .?'

The climbing jargon was not easy for the average person. The families were still learning it. How were they killed? K2 was tricky. The accident had happened in a remote part of the world. While the families were keen to know what happened, they simply couldn't process the information. But everyone knew roughly there was never good news with an avalanche.

"They died in that way. Believe me."

So, Kim re-emphasized that K2 was the most dangerous mountain, and the deaths were in the nature of K2 climbing. However, there were still so many unanswered questions, which made it even harder for the distraught families to understand. What happened?

Kim continued his explanation in tears.

"The summit was in sight. Because of the greed of it, we invited the disaster. If I could turn back time, I would."

And he showed some slides of the mountain and the accident scene.[240] K2 Accident Report by 2008 K2 Flying Jump K2 Expedition was projected by Shon Byung-Woo.

"The place of the accident was near the Bottleneck where the couloir on both sides covered by ice... It was sharply inclined. That was the place where most of the falling accidents occurred during the descent after summits or after giving up with exhaustion... They died by natural disaster... Let's accept the deaths as death."

It was Kim's desperate persuasion with sweat and tears.[241]

We've usually accepted these kinds of reports as fact or truth. But this time something was different. Comparing Wilco and Marco's accounts, Kim's account was sharply different in some events. That was one of the strange points for me about the story of the 2008 K2 disaster. Which one was right? Was Kim's explanation the true story? Or a fairy story? We should have a better picture.

While Kim was in the firing line, all his lieutenants were standing alongside. They were learning how to play the game. And the club members were backing Kim by remaining silent and saying nothing.

The team handed over to the families a red helmet and other personal belongings (the diaries via mail, later). In receiving these, it was certain for families that their father, husband or son had died.

In question time, somebody guided Kim and his colleagues to seats at the front table. Kim sat in the center. On his right was the No. 2 man Kim Seong-Sang and on his left Shon Byung-Woo. It was time for journalists' questions.

---

[240] http://www.nocutnews.co.kr/news/484415

[241] http://app.yonhapnews.co.kr/YNA/Basic/Article/ArticlePhoto/yibw_ showarticlephotopopup.aspx?contents_id=PYH20080813092100052

"Your explanation is not enough."

"Evidence, not emotion, is what guides us. Please, explain more."

They distrusted words rooted in the Himalaya cover-ups in the name of preserving mountaineering popularity. But Kim answered the questions sincerely. He repeatedly batted them all away. Knowing more about the disaster, more questions popped up. A journalist asked him:

"Seeing the other climbers' testimony from the other news sources, the disaster was blamed on the delay of rope-fixing and the Korean team's faults. How do you think?"

Kim denied this accusation:

"The testimonies of the survivors are not correct. The news content which came from foreign media sources is not correct. Many were twisted... Let me clear. They approached us earlier... Because of the lack of preparation by foreign teams, there was a chain of events that didn't go as planned. But now they are blaming us... For the sake of the dead members, I'll do everything possible to the end to restore their reputations."

In that way, the shattered Kim vowed to fight on.

On the evening news, *MBC-TV* aired what Kim had said about disaster. His statement was an effective use of the media to distort the facts. Whatever the facts were, they had already been buried under an avalanche of half truths cooked up by desperate climbers and speculative journalism on the K2 tragedy.

Sixty-four

Back in Islamabad, it was still August 13 (D+12), Wednesday. What was going on with the Norit team? The entire team was ready to meet with Gerard's family in the evening.

They gave Gerard's belongings, including his camera, to Annie and JJ. And then they tried to piece together what had happened to Gerard. Here again, the reality was a mystery to everyone. It was getting dark so they lit a candle. While Annie was talking about Gerard in tears, Pemba was struggling... to reveal a fact. Eventually, he came forward to make an important point.

"I didn't witness Gerard's death. But I got a second radio call from Sherpa Big Pasang. He informed me that he saw Gerard."

A second radio call? This was a different story to the teammates. Naturally, some confusion erupted among them. [242] Roeland responded that he had learned this different view of events at K2BC. Cas also expressed that he had another view on the death from Marco the other day. Norit climbers' views were divided over Gerard's death. Pemba continued:

"Two fresh Sherpas forced by Korean leader to reach Koreans, just top section of the couloir. And then they are descending together."

Two fresh Sherpas? And Cas said:

"I thought they were already dead, the three who were hanging, but probably they had been moving them."

Cas might have missed the point. Anyway, Pemba said:

"Yeah, then same time, three, four times, the serac fell down. Multi times serac..."

Multi times serac . . . ?!! The confused family couldn't get accurate information. It was unbelievable to see the extent to which opinions on the events were so divided. No one could shut down what Pemba had opened up. Pemba was a key eyewitness. He had seen events first-hand.

---

[242] p. 163-5, *The Time Has Come* by Damien O'Brien

Gerard's family could rely on Pemba's words, and Damien had recorded the meeting with his video camera. Come to think of it, only Pemba could have the authority in this matter. The grieving family could stand strong on Pemba's words.

"His words are trustworthy," they agreed.

"He holds the key to many people's questions."

The family invited the Norit team to Gerard's memorial service in County Limerick, Ireland, and before saying farewell, they had a photo session together.

Maarten of NLBC updated the Norit blog after the meeting:

> "The Norit K2 Expedition team had extensive meetings with the relatives of McDonnell in Pakistan, and the Dutch members will return home tomorrow Thursday, August 14th. The four Dutch team members will meet the press after their arrival in Amsterdam to talk about the expedition and the tragic developments during August 1–3."

Meanwhile, Alberto Zerain's team had arrived in Islamabad. Nazir Sabir conducted a thorough debrief with him:

> "I had a lengthy meeting with Mr Alberto of Spain, who was first on the summit that day at 3pm."

It was another attempt by Nazir, after his failed meeting with Korean and Norit teams.

Alberto Zerain's team was now waiting for a flight back to Spain.

Sixty-five

August 14, D+13, Thursday

It was Pakistan's Independence day and a public holiday. Gerard's family was on the flight back home.

In the morning, Norit team members were ready to go home, leaving from the Regency Hotel on the outskirts of Islamabad. Andrew Buncombe the Independent reporter described it:

> "Close to the hotel's large glass doors is a huge pile of climbing equipment—tents, sleeping bags, crampons and other hardware brought back from the mountain. For now, they sit drinking tea, tending to their injuries and thinking about what has happened. Much of the time is spent updating their expedition's website and speaking with officials and relatives of those who died. They are determined to try to provide as much insight as they can.
>
> "The sunburnt climbers are friendly if, unsurprisingly, somewhat shell-shocked. After all, they have survived while so many of their friends perished. But even at this point, it is clear that the experience will only deter them from climbing for a while. To a non-addict, the lure of this high-altitude drug appears monstrous, unfathomable.
>
> "Wilco the expedition leader suggests that while McDonnell's death is a tragedy for his family, for climbers it is an acceptable way to die. When he speaks, he does so very matter-of-factly. There is no false bravado. "It's hard to believe, but our passion is in the mountains," he says. "If you die in the mountains... it happens at the highlight of your life... You are living for your passion. If you die when you are 90, then that is great. But for mountaineers it's acceptable to die where your heart is."

All the Norit team members were torn apart. Pemba and Mark had left for their home countries. Other Norit members would leave soon.

Back at K2BC, the Americans Mike Farris, Dave Watson, Chuck Boyd and George Dijmarescu were still there with two Nepali Sherpas. They were still hoping for a K2 summit bid.

On his rest days, George had followed the news of the K2 disaster with his laptop. He thought some media had gone too far and posted his thoughts on his blog.

> "As I look at the whole picture, I anticipate more erroneous reporting, a gross disservice to the events that unfolded on K2 these past few weeks."

He noticed that the online climbing magazine *Outside*, which would publish a special report on the disaster. But he was disappointed to know that Michael Kodas, the author of the book *High Crime*, would write the report.

At 10.30pm Netherlands time, Norit Netherland members arrived at Schiphol airport. Wilco was still in a wheelchair. Everyone could feel how terrible his suffering was. Wilco had changed into his favorite orange jacket with the sponsor's logos.

All members had attended the press conference. But Wilco was the main speaker. His descent tale was an epic story.[243]

The next day, Wilco and Cas were going to fly to Ireland to attend Gerard's memorial.

In Serbia, the K2 team turned up at home club[244] and had the press conference about the Dren's death. The main reporter was Iso Planic.[245]

August 15, D+14, Friday

In Spain, Alberto and his teammates Aitor Las Hayas and Juan Carlos González were interviewed by El Correo Digital.[246]

Though they returned home, they realized the media had harshly criticized the K2 disaster every day. They quickly called a press conference at Alberto's hometown so they could remodel the mood by explaining their views on the events.

---

[243] www.youtube.com/watch?/v=IFwRPQCAHnA

[244] http://www.subotica.info/2008/08/14/docek-na-aerodromu

[245] http://www.subotica.info/2008/08/14/srbija-k2-2008-press-konferencija

[246] http://www.explorersweb.com/oceans/news.php?id=17497

"Don't look for anyone to blame. Perished climbers deserve respect," they said.

I've been hearing that song since 1976. Still, the same song. And Juan Carlos González stressed that:

"When you hear of such a drama, you try to imagine the situation and think of what could have gone wrong... But you mustn't put the blame on anyone. Mountain climbing demands making decisions, and sometimes these can be the wrong ones—but at 8000m it is very difficult to evaluate the situation. There have been many false comments published about the ones who died. They were all experienced climbers, and we all expose ourselves when climbing. People who perished (on K2) deserve respect, not frivolous accusations."

Sixty-six

August 16, D+15, Saturday

In Korea, the tragic news was hard to tell children. A "physical good-bye" can make the grief process easier. A farewell service was conducted by the mountaineering club Kafgyungnam.

At 10am, the farewell service was held in a solemn mood. The victims' families were already crying. For the victims' children, the ceremony itself was a sad event.

"Dad can't come back. We can't see Dad anymore."

"How can I live without you...?"

All seats in the service room at Kum Kang Hospital were taken. But seeing the packed room and hearing sugar-coated tributes didn't comfort the families. Again, many presses were present. It was hopeless for the families.

Go was not there. When Kim had recorded the summit video footage, she said to her colleagues Hwang, Park and Jumic "Well done, thank you so much for your hard work!" But, now, where was she? She had disappeared. Not a single representative from Kolon Sport was there.

Wasn't the blue-chip company Kolon Sport the main sponsor for Go's fourteen 8000er race? And wasn't Kim her manager? March 26, 2008 marked three years since Kim had made his contract with Kolon Sport.[247] The deal paved the way for him to carry out his K2 project using Kafgyungnam. The Korean team's 2008 K2 expedition was Go's K2 project, which meant Kolon was backing it as a big sponsor.

Everyone knows the brand war in the Korean market. The companies have advertised and promoted their products like mad, but when one of their climbers dies they claim the climber should have known better. Likewise, the K2 expedition was part of a big deal and the team paid a

---

[247] http://www.mountaintv.co.kr/board/mtnews/view.asp?tn=b_news&idx=98&page=11&search_part=&search_text=

high price for the brand. Now, where were the Kolon people, including Go? Absent! The company refused to stand behind climbers!

Could the company really avoid its duties? If the company was making its money of the backs of climbers who were dying, then the company had a moral responsibility. A corporate responsibility, as well. Kolon should have shared the responsibility for the climbers' deaths.

This action was also part of the culture in Korean mountaineering society. Sponsors distanced themselves from their corporate responsibilities whenever these kinds of accidents occurred.

In such an environment, wouldn't it lead expedition members to choose to hide the truth? We should know better. Since Korea is a collective society, it is easier to be a club first.

During the funeral service, Kim read his script about the accident. Lee In-Jeong the president of KAF gave the usual good eulogy.

Before the three photo-frames were taken out, visitors and families—one by one, or in groups—had time to present flowers in front of them. The farewell moved families to tears.[248] After returning to their seats there were lots of raw, emotional scenes again. The cameras inched closer as more and more of the families broke down while people were still parading to present flowers. It was Hwang's son whose cries of grief captured the unimaginable agony of the family.[249]

At the last part of the ceremony, the presenter asked the victim's families:

"Please stand up, and give thank you bows to the visitors."

The families felt peer-pressured by the power of the many. But Park's mother didn't stand up, to the end. Her world had collapsed with the loss of her son. This was more of a show than anything else and the club would easily move to the next phase. Although victims' families were key players in this disastrous event, they could do nothing against this system in Korea. People, members, clubs were all above them.

The adventure was too dangerous to be covered by insurance. The disaster left victims' families crippled. The kids were to be raised by mothers and relatives. How about widows and the elderly mother? A local appeal "Let's help the families!" was made by GyeongNam province people.

---

[248] http://kr.channel.pandora.tv/channel/video.ptv?ch_userid=yunhap
&prgid=32804394&categid=1608216&page=3223&ref=ch&lot=cthum2_1_2
[249] http://himalayaz.co.kr/boards/free.asp?p_a=view&cid=2587&page=160

Back in Islamabad, the rest of the K2 climbers were still arriving at the ACP one by one, or in a groups for debriefs. Nick Rice dropped into the Club for his debrief and picked up Hugues' K2 summit certificate. Chhiring also got his summit certificate after debriefing.[250]

The Norwegians Lars and Øystein had also debriefed at the Alpine Club. Øystein got Cecilia's summit certificate instead.[251]

After that, they had an interview with Karrar, the ExWeb's Pakistan correspondent. Although it was the first and the Norwegian team's only interview, there was a timeline given in the report on the descents from the K2 summit. Any information on what had happened when during the descent would be helpful in solving the mystery surrounding August 2's fatal accidents. Other teams have not been testified yet in detail.

Then, Cecilia went to be with Rolf's mom and dad. The family's spokesperson announced a memorial service for Rolf in Stavanger Cathedral, Friday, August 22 at 12 noon.

August 17, D+16, Sunday

At Kilcornan, Ireland, a memorial service called 'Celebration Of Ger's Life' was held by his family and friends. It was a rainy day, but over 1000 people paid their respect to Gerard McDonnell at the mass. Norit team members including a Norit spokeperson were in the front seats.

The President Mary McAleese and Taoiseach Brian Cowen were represented at the ceremony by their aides-de-camp. Gerard's brother JJ made a speech:

> "He had a passion for life that made all our lives fuller... He wanted us all to share in his joy for life but what all of us will miss the most will be his big hugs."

At the end of the service, the family released doves into the sky.

---

[250] http://www.8264.net/html/fair-events/other-events/200808/18-2028.html
[251] http://www.summitpost.org/norvegian-k2-expedition-2008/479588

Sixty-seven

August 18, D+17, Monday
Nazir Sabir Sabir—president of the Alpine Club of Pakistan issued an open letter and sent it to the Himalaya mountaineering world.[252]

"Greetings from Islamabad.

The recent tragedy on K2 is a most unfortunate incident in which eleven precious lives were lost above 8000m. This has been another deadly incident in the history of K2, one which grieves all of us here in Pakistan. One Serbian and a Pakistani died on the way up, and all of the others died on their return from the summit. Most of them became weak due to exposure, as they were forced to spend the night of August 1, 2008 out in the open above the Bottleneck—higher than 8200m, with temperatures below -25°C wind chill making it even worse.

From a climber's point of view, I think they all made several mistakes: for example, making an agreement on a joint final summit push with over two dozen people at the same time, or depending on others for fixing ropes above 8000m. The worst part was a lack of timely crucial decision making in addition to trying to reach the summit so very late in the day. Although most of them had a sound climbing background, there were some climbers who were lacking the crucial extra energy, experience for survival and technical ability to cope with this kind of situation.

We know that a few survivors are trying to blame some other climbers, local crew and others. They also seem to be throwing responsibility elsewhere, claiming that ropes were fixed much below the Bottleneck on easier ground, and they had to replace them, which made them late in reaching the summit. They also blame some of the high altitude porters, but it is evident that all

[252] http://www.alpinist.com/doc/web08x/newswire-letter-nazir-sabir

the teams are deeply divided on where to throw the blame for various issues. This is unfortunate, and is often the case when tragedies of this magnitude occur; this kind of blame game to me seems unfair. I acknowledge the fact that we humans often find it hard to make accurate decisions when embroiled in such situations and at this altitude we tend to make mistakes. The Sherpas and the high altitude porters can't be expected to play the role of fixing the ropes and camps on higher ground on K2. Commercial climbing has no place on K2 like on easier mountains like Broad Peak, G2 or even Everest.

Meanwhile, we have been meeting the returning climbers who were part of the dilemma and were higher up on K2. There are obvious differences on several issues among the many parties on the mountain.

I had a lengthy meeting with Mr. Alberto of Spain, who was first on the summit that day at 3 p.m. It seems the last person who left the summit was around 9:30 p.m. It was suicidal to continue climbing toward the summit of K2 when they had seen the route conditions around the Bottleneck, and had even witnessed people dying earlier in the day. There have been several mentions of people losing their senses during the descent—at night, and out of oxygen.

The Serbian mountaineer Mr. Dren Mandic lost his life when he slipped from the lower icy slope of the Bottleneck. This fatal accident took place around 11:12 a.m. on Friday, August 1 as a much worse omen on a summit day. His body was found fifteen minutes later by his two teammates and one of their Pakistani high altitude porters. It has been said that the Pakistani climber Jehan Baig was returning due to fatigue and some illness. He also took part in retrieving the body of Dren and suddenly slipped down eastern icy slopes of K2. The Serbian team leader, Mr. Milivoj Erdeljan, issued a statement with further details that can be read on EverestNews.com.[253]

This incident was discussed at a high-level meeting held at the Ministry of Tourism. Both Dutch survivors Wilco van Rooijen and Cas van de Gevel, the Korean climbers, their LO Capt. Azim and their Sherpas also were present at this condolence meeting.

---

[253] http://www.everestnews.com/pak2008/k22008sadnews081220080101.
htm

The Secretary of Tourism will put together a team to conduct a thorough fact-finding investigation consisting of both officials from Ministry of Tourism and the Alpine Club of Pakistan to probe into the drama on K2.

With best regards,

Nazir Sabir

It was not a short letter. There were confusion and complexities, but they were solvable. All the complicated mysteries surrounding the 2008 K2 disaster and deaths should have been solved, if it was not an act of God, for justice and for the families to have proper closure.

However, who would do that when the Pakistani authority had failed to handle it adequately? Who would undertake that task when each authority had failed?

•

The 2008 K2 Disaster has never been properly investigated.

About the Author

Jun Ki Lim is a Korean-born New Zealander, armchair climber and amateur writer. He's also the author of *The Story Of New Zealand* (Korean edition). Married, with two adult children, he loves to travel and read.

Cover Photo: The helicopter scene taken by a trekker on August 5, 2008. It was a great escape from K2BC after the August 1 and 2 disaster unfolded. (*Courtesy* Man Su Kim)

Rear Photo: The next morning's rescue situation at 8am, August 2, 2008. (*Credit* Lars Nessa Flato)